Hear It and Sing It!
Exploring the Blues

JUDY NIEMACK

ISBN 9 781458 412034
HL00230106

Copyright © 2012 Second Floor Music
International Copyright Secured   All Rights Reserved   Printed in U.S.A.
Second Floor Music, 130 West 28th Street, floor 2, New York, N.Y. 10001 U.S.A.
www.secondfloormusic.com • www.jazzleadsheets.com

A Don Sickler Production
SECOND FLOOR MUSIC

EXCLUSIVELY DISTRIBUTED BY
HAL•LEONARD CORPORATION
7777 W. BLUEMOUND RD. P.O. BOX 13819 MILWAUKEE, WI 53213

JUDY NIEMACK'S HEAR IT AND SING IT! EXPLORING THE BLUES
CD TRACK LISTINGS

CD #1
1. *A Shot of Blues Juice*
2. accompaniment only
3. *Basic Blues Workout*
4. accompaniment only
5. Pentatonic Minor Scale
6. Blues Scale
7. Hear It and Sing It: Pentatonic Minor & Blues
8. Pentatonic Major Scale
9. Major Blues Scale
10. Etude: Pentatonic Major & Major Blues
11. Alternating Thirds & Sevenths
12. Third & Seventh of each chord
13. accompaniment only
14. Hear It and Sing It with Guitar
15. *Since You've Gone*
16. Judy's scat solo
17. Mark Murphy's scat solo
18. Jamming with Darmon Meader
19. accompaniment only
20. *Something to Say*
21. Judy's scat solo
22. accompaniment only
23. *The Count Is Back*
24. Trading twos with Sheila Jordan
25. accompaniment only
26. *Jazz Blues Workout*
27. Developing Motifs
28. accompaniment only
29. *New Concept (for a Blue Planet)*
30. accompaniment only

CD #2
1. *In Flight*
2. Judy & Sheila Jordan trade fours
3. accompaniment only
4. *Summer Blues*
5. accompaniment only
6. *Ice White Blues*
7. accompaniment only
8. *Sheila's Blues*
9. accompaniment only
10. *Run Home*
11. accompaniment only
12. *Eros*
13. accompaniment only
14. *The Meeting*
15. accompaniment only
16. *Blues That Soothe My Soul*
17. accompaniment only
18. *Over the Brink*
19. accompaniment only

legend:

1 – 30 CD #1 (square track numbers)

① – ⑲ CD #2 (round track numbers)

1 ① illustrated by vocalist (black track number in white)

2 ❸ accompaniment only (white track number in black)

CDs are inside the back cover

Judy Niemack's Hear It and Sing It! Exploring the Blues

4	Preface	70	**Chapter 6: Bird Blues**
5	About the Book	71	Guide Tones
		72	*In Flight*
6	**Chapter 1: Getting Started with Blues**	76	Judy and Sheila trading fours
7	*A Shot of Blues Juice*		
10	12-measure Blues	78	**Chapter 7: Blues Scale on Standards**
12	The Lyric Form	79	*Summer Blues*
12	Call and Response in Blues Lyrics		
		82	**Chapter 8: Blues with a Bridge**
13	**Chapter 2: Learning to Improvise**	82	*Ice White Blues*
13	Four Steps to Singing Blues Changes		
14	*Basic Blues Workout*	86	**Chapter 9: Original Blues Lyrics**
16	Scales to Know	86	*Sheila's Blues*
17	Pentatonic Minor Scale		
17	Blues Scale	89	**Chapter 10: Vocalese Blues**
19	Pentatonic Major Scale	90	*Run Home*
19	Major Blues Scale		
22	Movement of Thirds and Sevenths	94	**Chapter 11: Odd-Meter Blues**
24	Hear It and Sing It with Guitar	95	*Eros*
27	Scat Syllables	100	*The Meeting*
29	Pronunciation Guide for Scat Syllables		
		104	**Chapter 12: Chromatic Melody Blues**
30	**Chapter 3: Blues Riffs and Riff Blues**	104	*Blues That Soothe My Soul*
31	*Since You've Gone*		
34	Scatting *Since You've Gone*	106	**Chapter 13: Simultaneous Improvising**
36	Mark Murphy's scat solo	106	*Over the Brink*
40	Jamming with Darmon Meader		
		108	**Chapter 14: Voices in Blues**
45	**Chapter 4: Minor Blues**		
46	*Something to Say*	122	Appendix
48	Soloing on Minor Blues	123	Essential Listening List
52	*The Count Is Back*	124	Blues at a Jam Session
55	Trading twos with Sheila Jordan	125	Blues with Lyrics
		126	Riff Blues
58	**Chapter 5: Jazz Blues**	126	Vocalese Blues
59	Jazz Blues Progressions	127	Resources
60	Singing the Changes		
62	*Jazz Blues Workout*	129	About Judy Niemack
64	Developing Motifs	131	Judy Niemack's Selected Discography
67	*New Concept (for a Blue Planet)*		
68	Trading fours with the drummer	134	Acknowledgments

Copyright © 2012 SECOND FLOOR MUSIC

Preface

My love of blues was kindled at the age of twelve, when I began taking piano lessons from a woman who lived down the block. She had the good judgment to teach me Henry Mancini's *Baby Elephant Walk,* and I would practice for hours, relishing the thundering boogie-woogie groove in the left hand. It wasn't until years later that I realised it was a blues.

As a teenager, the first live blues concert I heard live was the Muddy Waters Band opening for The Grateful Dead—within minutes the crowd was up and dancing. The next day, the guitarist in our high school rock band brought in a recording of *Stormy Monday* by the Allman Brothers Band, and we were hooked. We decided to play it in our next concert. Janis Joplin's *Turtle Blues* and Koko Taylor's *I'm a Woman* were next. I'd never sung anything with so much raw emotion before, and the morning after the performance, my voice was gone. I wanted to keep singing blues, but needed to find a way to do it without hurting myself. Working with a classical voice teacher, I began to develop a technique that would allow me to sing in any style.

Blues led me to jazz, and my interest in jazz led to lessons in improvisation with saxophonist Warne Marsh, with whom I transcribed and sang blues solos by Charlie Parker, Miles Davis, and John Coltrane. When I discovered that Billie Holiday named Bessie Smith as one of her influences, I started to listen to the classic blues singers, worked back even further to the country blues singers. I started teaching and began to compile a list of jazz repertoire for my students. I was surprised that so many of the songs I loved were based on some type of blues, from Annie Ross's *Twisted* to Miles Davis's *All Blues,* to Charles Mingus's *Goodbye Pork Pie Hat.*

Blues began as African-American music, born out of the suffering caused by slavery and its aftermath in the United States. Blues may appear to be simple, but in the diverse styles that have evolved since their beginnings, musicians have found an incredible freedom of expression. Blues diva Ruth Brown said, "Nowadays, anybody who has a need, and can find the need, they can sing the blues." Recently, on tour in Beijing, I passed a bar and heard what sounded like a Muddy Waters recording blaring out into the street. I looked inside, and saw a Chinese guitarist with a waist-length braid, singing like a Delta bluesman. My work has allowed me to travel the world and experience music's astounding capacity to unify people across cultural and language barriers. Blues is a powerful example of a music that began with humble roots and has rapidly become a worldwide influence.

I hope you enjoy **Hear It and Sing It! Exploring the Blues**.

Sincerely,

Judy Niemack

ABOUT THE BOOK

Hear It and Sing It! Exploring the Blues was created for people who just love to sing, as well as for teachers and students in high school or university vocal jazz programs. It includes a step-by-step process for understanding blues lyrics, forms, harmony, scales and improvisation, with brand new lyrics to compositions by such jazz masters as Dexter Gordon, Norman Simmons, Johnny Griffin, Julian Priester and Gigi Gryce. As in my first vocal book, *Hear It and Sing It! Exploring Modal Jazz,* learning by singing is an essential part of my method, and the musicians playing on the recordings are world-class. You can improve as a vocalist, improviser and blues interpreter by singing along with the recorded tracks on the included CDs, or dive more deeply into the world of blues with the information and exercises provided in the book. The music itself was painstakingly transcribed, so that you can read what you'll hear on the recordings. Clear lead sheets make it easy to perform the songs with a band or combo, on your own, or in the vocal jazz program at your High School or University.

You'll start off by hearing A *Shot of Blues Juice,* a finger-snapping tune that I wrote with pianist Norman Simmons. I have provided you with phrases to repeat that function as a vocal warm-up. Four important blues scales are covered next, then basic blues harmonies. You can try call-and-response patterns with blues guitar, and then "Hear It and Sing It" exercises with each of the vocalists on a variety of exciting accompaniment tracks. You'll hear an example of how blue notes can be used on jazz standards, and have a chance to practice trading "twos" and "fours" with different instruments. By repeating what you hear, you will start to internalize the harmonic progressions and scales used in improvisation.

Exploring the Blues introduces a brand-new repertoire of songs, including riff blues, minor blues, jazz blues, blues with a bridge, blues that tell a story (illustrated beautifully by Sheila Jordan), vocalese blues and odd-meter blues. Every song on the included CDs comes as a lead sheet or transcription with notated solos. They can be used as exercises or performed. Finally, "Voices in Blues" presents an overview of blues and blues singers from their early days up until the emergence of jazz, and is followed by an appendix with extensive listening and repertoire suggestions.

A note on the transcriptions and lead sheets. Musical notation is limited just like language; it isn't possible to notate every nuance and inflection used in blues and jazz. Up until now, there has been no standard way of writing scat syllables. However, in this book we've done our best to give you clear, accurate and understandable written versions of what we are doing. When you see **vocal lead sheet** on the music, you'll find the original rhythm, melody and harmony of the song. The recorded version may sound slightly different, depending on the interpretation of the vocalist. I've interpreted the songs in my own style, and you can do the same as you practice with the accompaniment tracks. We have also included detailed **transcriptions** of the rhythmic accents and phrasing that our singers used on the CDs. A chart explaining how the vowels in the written scat solos sound can be found on page 29, in case you are working on them without the recordings.

Chapter 1: Getting Started with Blues

Let's start with singing a blues. At the beginning of any practice session, it's important to warm up, so try *A Shot of Blues Juice* to get your voice in gear.

Since your body is your instrument, warming up for singing includes stretching. Stand up with your feet shoulder-width apart, and reach up towards the ceiling, inhaling deeply. Grasp your hands together, palms up, and hold for a moment. Then exhale slowly, lowering your arms to the sides, as you bring the shoulder blades back and down, finally letting your arms hang comfortably at your sides. Let your chin drop to your chest, then look to the right, center, left, return to center, and up again. Look straight ahead, then over your right shoulder as far as you can, then return to center, look over your left shoulder as far as you can, and finally straight ahead again.

With your mouth closed, slowly roll your tongue around your gums, feeling the outside of your teeth as you roll around to the right and then to the left. Repeat in each direction five times, then relax. Squeeze your eyes shut and scrunch your face into a knot, pursing your lips, and hold a couple of seconds. Then stretch your mouth open as wide as possible, opening your eyes widely and sticking your tongue out as far as possible. Relax. Roll your shoulders back and down a few times, and shake any stiffness out of your hands, legs and feet. Ready to move? Feel the energy flowing as you let your body sway to the music or walk around the room in tempo.

After the lyrics, I've recorded a "hear it and sing it" exercise. Just repeat what you hear me singing; I've started with simple phrases that gradually increase in range and complexity, so that, by the end of the song, you'll be ready to practice with the accompaniment track..

A Shot of Blues Juice

Instrumentally known as "Blue Juice"

vocal lead sheet
B♭

Music by Norman Simmons
Lyric by Judy Niemack

Medium swing (♩ = ca. 112)

Lyrics:

1. Let's start with a shot of blues juice and pour it out ev-'ry day. Just sway to the band and hang loose, you'll nat'-ral-ly swing that way. Time to be cool, time to re-lax, we're gon-na play.

2. You might feel a great temp-ta-tion to kick off your shoes and move. With one sip of our li-ba-tion, there's noth-ing you've got to prove. Time to be cool, time to re-lax, we're gon-na groove.

to hear it and sing it next page

Coda: Time to breathe in, time to let go, sing-in' the blues.

Copyright © 1976 (renewed 2004), 2007, 2011 Second Floor Music

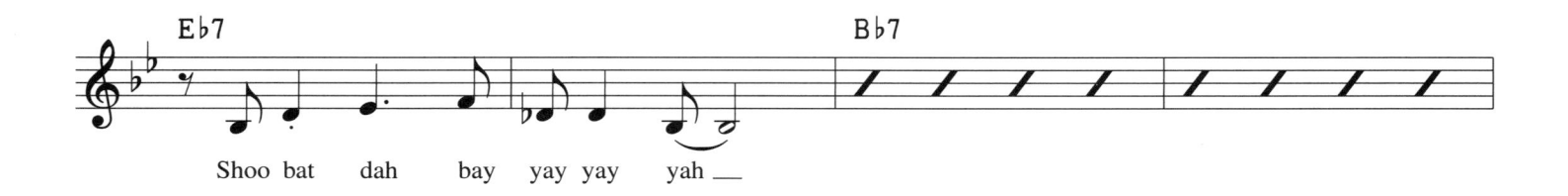

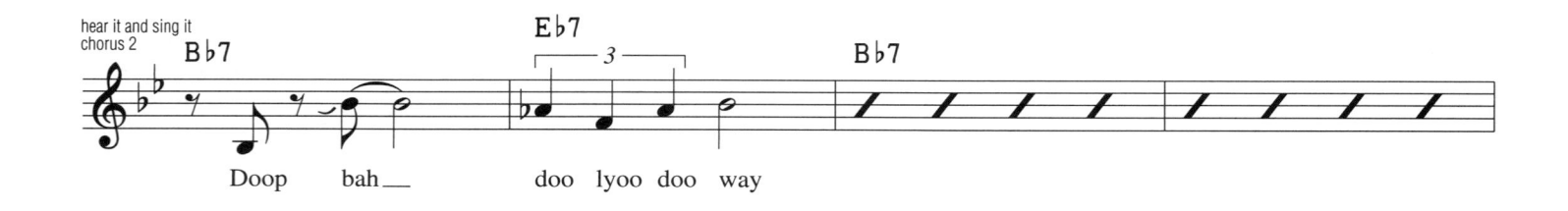

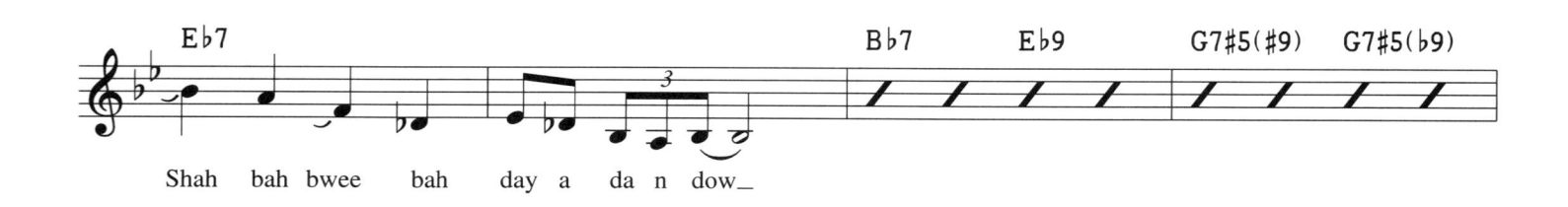

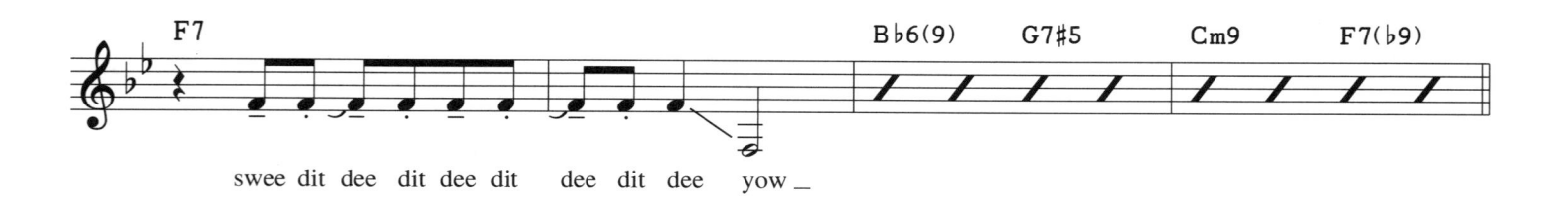

8   Chapter 1: Getting Started with Blues

hear it and sing it
chorus 1

Shoob - bay   doot   doo way __

Shoo bat   dah   bay   yay yay   yah __

Shoop   bah   doo lyoo doo wee __

hear it and sing it
chorus 2

Doop   bah __   doo lyoo doo way

Shah   bah bwee   bah   day a   da n   dow __

swee dit dee dit dee dit   dee dit dee   yow __

hear it and sing it
chorus 3

Shoop beh dit n day day shoop beh dit n day day___

Shoop beh dit n dee ba bo bway ow___

Shap bah vah veely oo vee dow___

hear it and sing it
chorus 4

Shap bah___ vwee dee doo yow___

Shoop bay doot day doot day doo doo dee doot dwee doot n dee yow

Sha yah bah bwee buh dooly oo bay n dee dow___

D.S. al ⊕
sing second lyric

You

In its early days, blues was a kind of folk music, sung by a solo musician who accompanied himself on guitar, harmonica or a homemade string instrument. The form changed according to the whim of the performer, since there was no need to play the same way each time. As blues became a popular song form, it eventually became available in sheet music, and the 12-measure form, consisting of three stanzas of four measures, became standard. Although blues are occasionally played in 8-measure (*Heartbreak Hotel*) or 16-measure (*Watermelon Man*) forms, the 12-measure (or 12-bar) blues progression is still the most common form.

12-measure Blues

The original 12-measure blues harmony was limited to the basic European chordal pattern made up of three dominant seventh chords*, based on the tonic, or first degree of the key, the sub-dominant, or fourth degree, and the dominant, or fifth degree (I - IV - I - V - I). The harmonic movement of the basic blues progression on the next page is written in Roman numerals below the chord symbols.

---

* Dominant seventh chords consist of the root, third, fifth and lowered seventh. The root is the lowest note of a chord, and corresponds to its letter name. C7 = C, E, G, B♭.

Notice the harmonic movement in each line of the blues progression:

tonic (I) sometimes with subdominant in bar two
subdominant (IV) sometimes back to tonic
dominant (V) sometimes via subdominant back to tonic

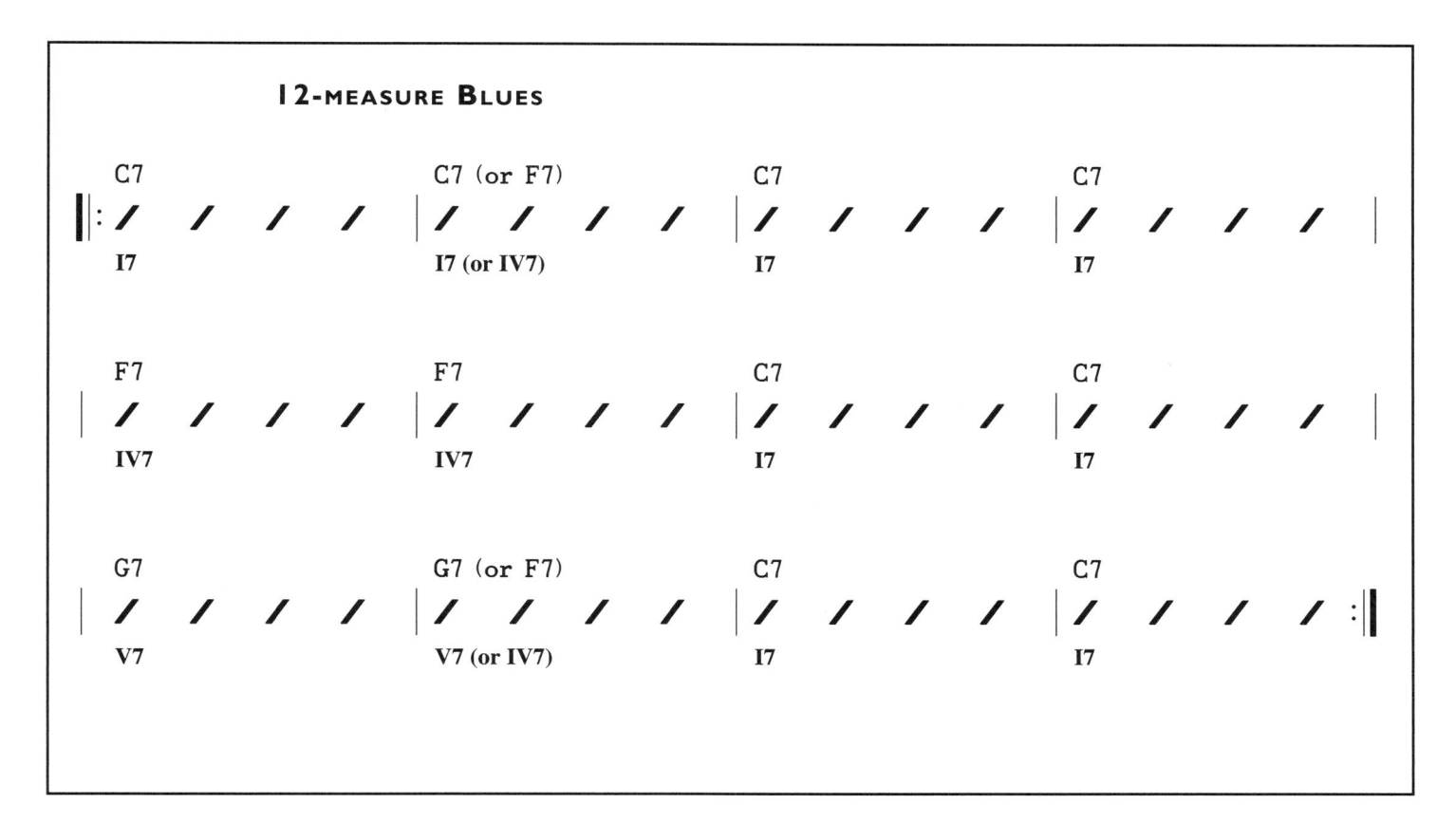

12-MEASURE BLUES

C7	C7 (or F7)	C7	C7
I7	I7 (or IV7)	I7	I7

F7	F7	C7	C7
IV7	IV7	I7	I7

G7	G7 (or F7)	C7	C7
V7	V7 (or IV7)	I7	I7

THE LYRIC FORM

The original lyric form of the blues was probably a single line, repeated three times, or an A - A - A form. It was only later that the current, most common structure—a line, repeated once with variations, followed by a single line conclusion, or A - A - B—became standard, as in *St. Louis Blues* and many others.

> I hate's to see dat ev'nin' sun go down
> Hate's to see dat ev'nin' sun go down
> 'Cause ma baby, she done lef' dis town
>
> If I feel tomorrow lak ah feel today
> Feel tomorrow lak ah feel today
> I'll pack up my trunk, and make ma git away
>
> *St. Louis Blues*, W.C. Handy

12-measure blues lyrics are often written in loosely interpreted traditional English "iambic pentameter" (ta-Dum, ta-Dum, ta-Dum, ta-Dum, ta-Dum).

> The sun will shine in my back door someday
> The sun will shine in my back door someday
> March winds will come, blow all my blues away
>
> *I Know You Rider*, Traditional

CALL AND RESPONSE IN BLUES LYRICS

Like many African tribal songs and work songs of the slaves, blues follow a call-and-response pattern. The first four measures form a statement that is repeated with variations in the second four measures, and the statement is answered or resolved in the last four measures.

> (Call) Since you've gone, I'm spending every night with the blues,
> (Call) Since you've gone, I'm spending every nights with the blues,
> (Response) Can't go on, 'cause there's no end in sight to these dues.

There's also an interior call and response pattern in each four measure phrase. Since the lyrics don't take up all the space, there's room for an instrumental response at the end of each line, usually played on the guitar. The response often overlaps the end of the phrase and the next phrase begins before the instrumental response is finished, creating a counter melodic effect. Sometimes the singer answers himself with "Lord, Lord!" or by repeating the last words of the phrase, for example "I hate to see the evening sun go down, oh yes, the sun go down."

Chapter 2: Learning to Improvise

Improvisation is an important part of the blues. When a jazz or blues singer improvises a melody without words, it's called "scat singing." When you scat, you're free to improvise a new melody and syllables to go with it. You'll find out more about scat syllables in the next chapter, but first let's look at a way to prepare you to improvise. After learning the melody and lyrics, create a mental picture of the form and the harmonic structure by "singing the changes."

Four Steps to Learning Basic Blues Changes

Jazz musicians call the chords to a song the chord "progression" or chord "changes." Here's a way to internalize the basic blues changes so that you'll always know exactly where you are.

1. Sing the tonic or "root" of each chord. (Reminder: The root is the lowest note of a chord and corresponds to its letter name. For example, the root of F7 is F.)

2. Sing the root and third of each chord.

3. Sing the chord tones, root, third, fifth and seventh.

4. Sing a bass line by adding the sixth degree of the scale, as in the following example.

You can learn these four steps by singing the *Basic Blues Workout* on the next page. Practice first with the vocal track, and then with the accompaniment track, until you can sing it from memory.

14 Chapter 2: Learning to Improvise — Judy Niemack's *Hear It and Sing It! Exploring the Blues*

vocal lead sheet
B♭

BASIC BLUES WORKOUT 3 4

Judy Niemack

Slow Blues

Intro (Bass)

(musical notation: B♭7 | B♭7/D E♭7 E | F7 |)

roots

chorus 1

B♭7 | | | |

Doo doo — doo doo — doo doo — doo doo —

E♭7 | | B♭7 | |

doo doo — doo doo — doo doo — doo doo —

F7 | E♭7 | B♭7 | F7 |

doo doo — doo doo — doo doo — doo doo —

roots and thirds

chorus 2

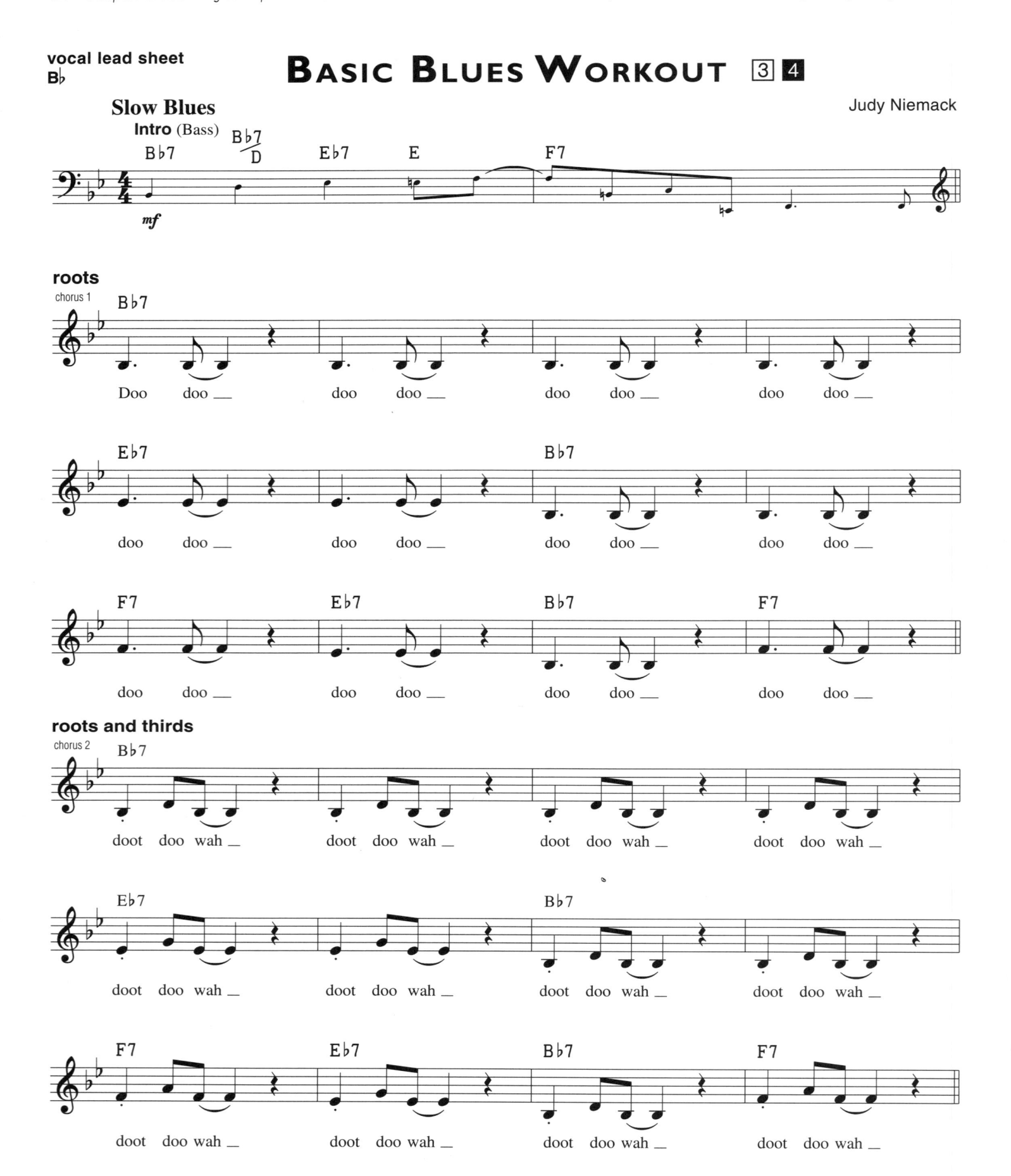

B♭7 | | | |

doot doo wah — doot doo wah — doot doo wah — doot doo wah —

E♭7 | | B♭7 | |

doot doo wah — doot doo wah — doot doo wah — doot doo wah —

F7 | E♭7 | B♭7 | F7 |

doot doo wah — doot doo wah — doot doo wah — doot doo wah —

Copyright © 2011 Second Floor Music

chord tones

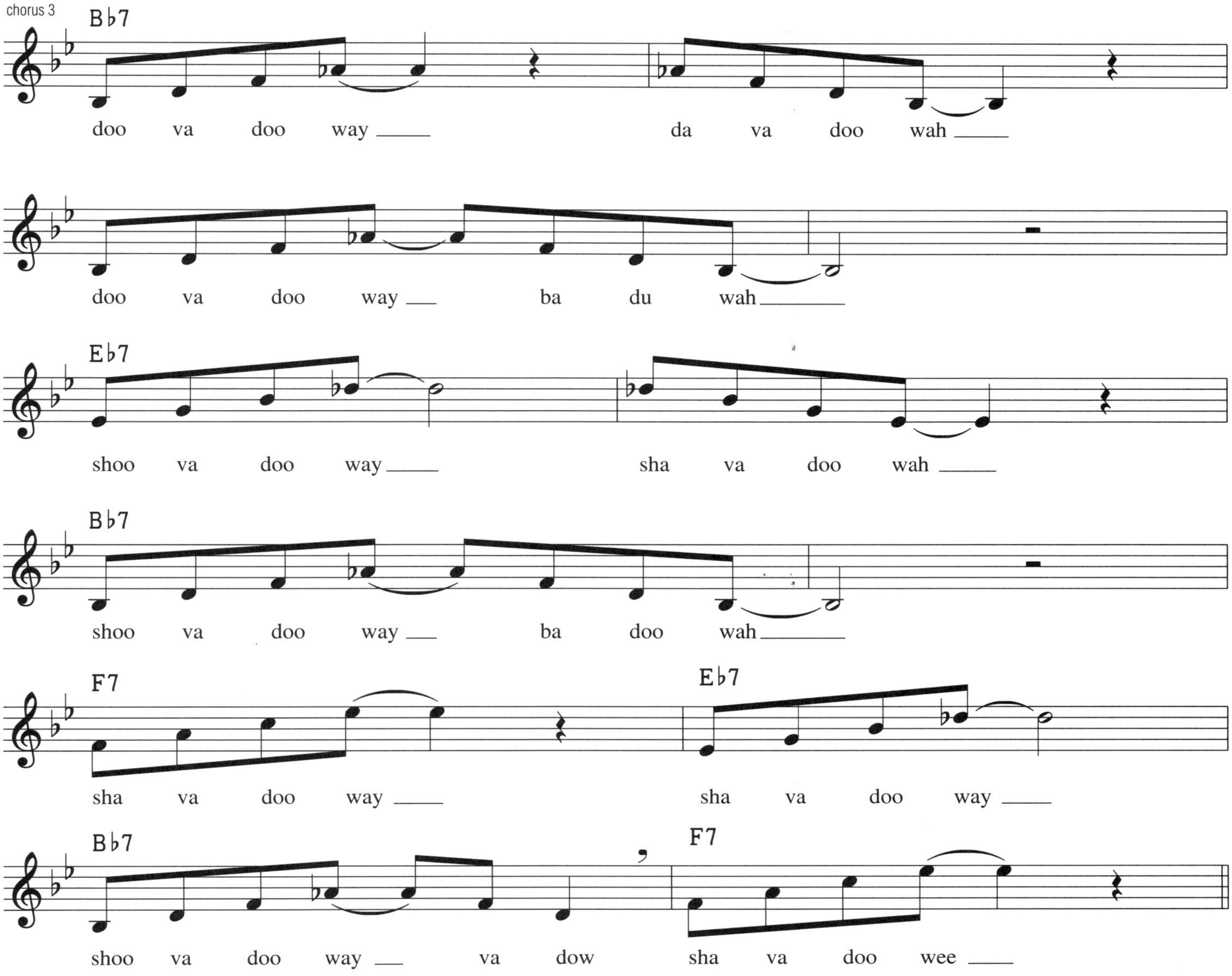

bass line

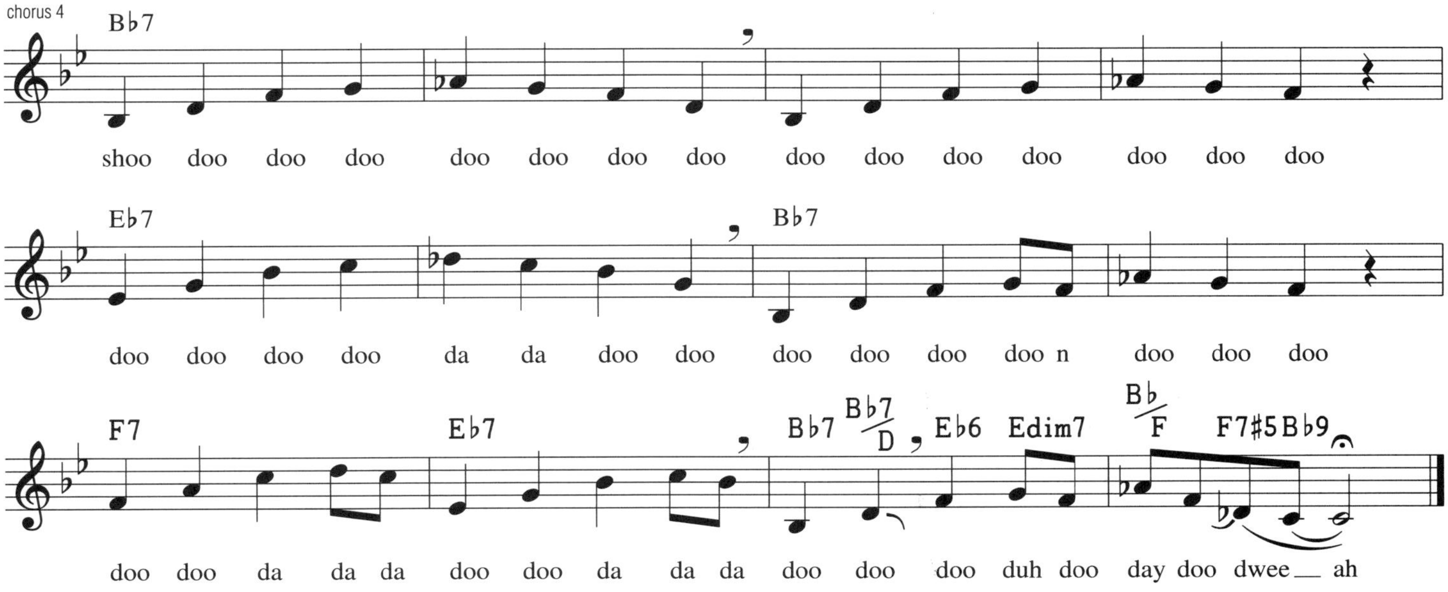

SCALES TO KNOW

Here are four scales commonly used in improvising on a basic blues progression. They are shown here in comparison to a major scale in the key of C.

C major scale
Cmaj7

1 2 3 4 5 6 7 8

C pentatonic minor scale
C7(♯9)

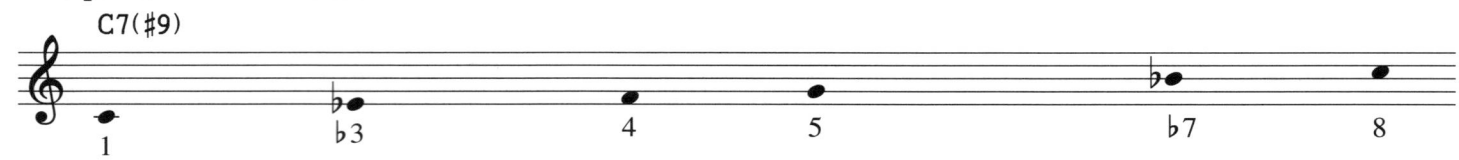

1 ♭3 4 5 ♭7 8

C blues scale
C7♭5(♯9)

1 ♭3 4 ♯4 5 ♭7 8

C pentatonic major scale
C9

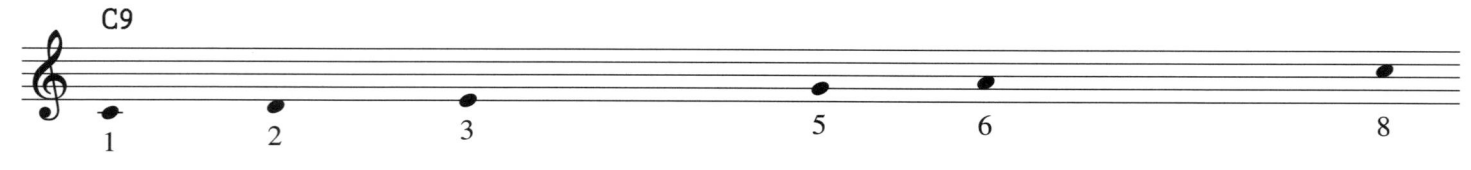

1 2 3 5 6 8

C major blues scale
C13

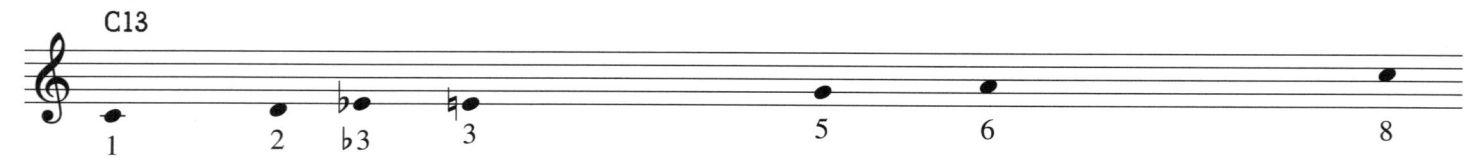

1 2 ♭3 3 5 6 8

The following examples are in the key of B♭, which falls in a range most comfortable for the majority of vocalists. First, listen to me sing each scale, then practice on your own as the piano continues.

B♭ pentatonic minor scale [5]

Da ya da ya dwee dow __ da ya da ya dwee dow __

The definition of a "pentatonic" scale is a five-tone scale. There are several different pentatonic scales, but the first one we'll look at is the pentatonic minor scale. It is the basis of the blues scale, which has just one additional note, the raised fourth degree. Like the blues scale, pentatonic minor can be used over the entire 12-measure blues chord progression.

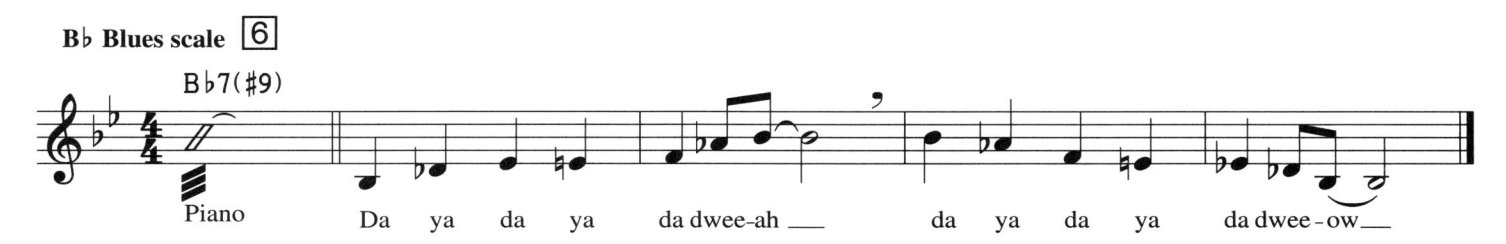

B♭ Blues scale [6]

Da ya da ya da dwee-ah __ da ya da ya da dwee-ow __

The blues scale (sometimes called the "minor blues scale") is the most important scale used in the blues. Most historians believe that it evolved out of the pentatonic minor scale, and was brought to America by slaves from West Africa, who spontaneously bent the third note of the scale, sliding between the minor and major third.

As you can see, if we compare it with a major scale, it has a lowered third, a lowered seventh and a raised fourth. These notes are called the "blue notes" which are "inflected" or bent notes; they're sung somewhere between the pitches surrounding them. The most commonly used blue note is the lowered third, next the lowered seventh, and finally the raised fourth. Being "dissonant" (outside of the scales that correspond to each chord), they create tension, tending to resolve to the "consonant" notes of the chord/scale. These swooping, sliding blue notes give the emotional, bittersweet color to the blues.

Here's some good news about the blues scale: since it can be used over the entire 12-measure blues progression, you don't have to change scales each time the chords change! But depending on which chord is being played, some notes will sound more dissonant than others and have a tendency to resolve differently.

18 Chapter 2: Learning to Improvise   Judy Niemack's *Hear It and Sing It! Exploring the Blues*

Notice the difference between the sound of the pentatonic minor
scale and the blues scale in these call and response exercises.

HEAR IT AND SING IT: PENTATONIC MINOR AND BLUES SCALES [7]

In a simple 12-measure blues, three different pentatonic major scales can be used. You can construct them beginning on the root of each of the three dominant chords. Using the scales that correspond to the chord changes, rather than just the blues scale, will give your solo more of a jazz sound.

B♭ pentatonic major scale [8]

(Musical notation: B♭7 chord, 4/4 time, Piano)
Da ya dwee ya dwee yah — da ya dee ya dwee dow —

The first page of the following Etude consists of melodies created from pentatonic major scales.

The major blues scale is a six-note scale. It is commonly used in country, bluegrass, rhythm & blues, swing or jump music. By adding the flat third or "blue note" to the major pentatonic scale, the music takes on a bluesy sound. In a simple 12-measure blues, three different major blues scales are used, corresponding to each of the three dominant chords. The minor third, or blue note, is dissonant, and is usually used as a passing note. That means it is not given much weight, and is merely an approach note to the note that follows it. If you hold it too long it sounds wrong. (Experiment and find out for yourself!)

B♭ major Blues scale [9]

(Musical notation: B♭7 chord, 4/4 time, Piano)
Da ya dwee ya da doo-wah — da ya dwee ya da doo-wah —

The second page of the following Etude consists of melodies created from major blues scales.

Notice the difference between the sound of the pentatonic major scale and the major blues scale in this Etude.

ETUDE: PENTATONIC MAJOR AND MAJOR BLUES SCALES

Slow Blues
Intro (Bass)

pentatonic major scale

chorus 1

Bb7 — Sha va da vay ___ vil ya va doo way ___

Bb7 — sha va doo vay va day va vay day ow ___

Eb7 — swee ___ va doo vee va da vway vo vo vo va doo vee va soo ___

Bb7 — ___ wee ___ vee ___ vow ___ see va da eh ___ ah

F7 — sha va da va vay ow Eb7 sha va da va day vee ay ow ___

Bb7 — ___ sha va doo voo deet dot F7 deet dweet dah

major blues scale

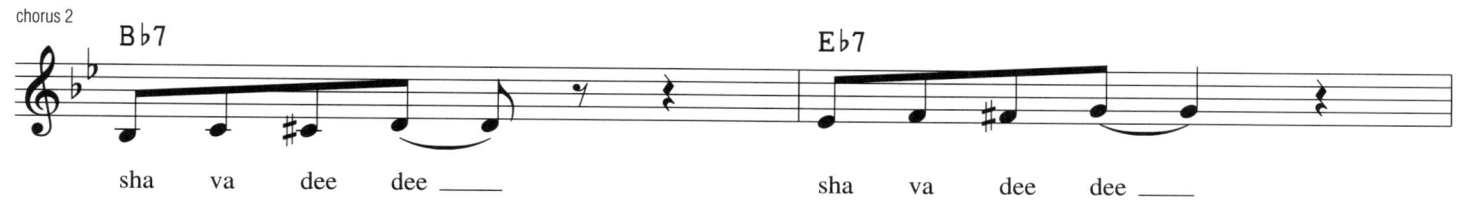

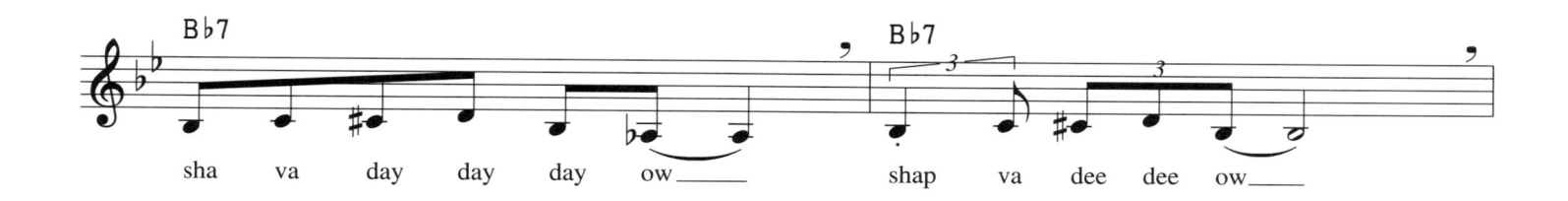

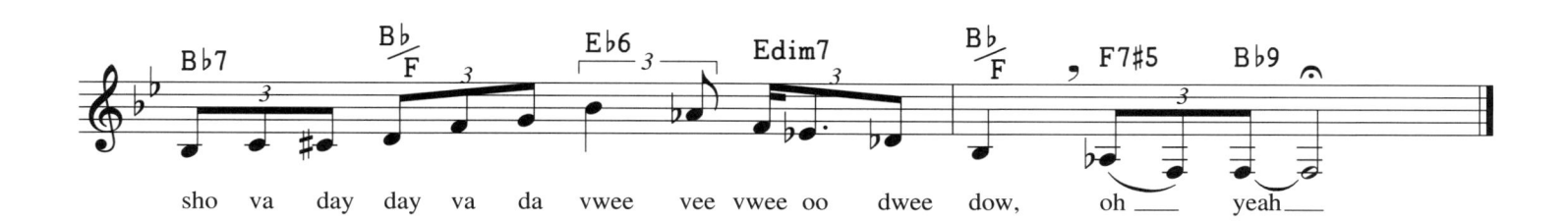

chorus 2

22 Chapter 2: Learning to Improvise   Judy Niemack's *Hear It and Sing It! Exploring the Blues*

The alteration of the third of the tonic scale from major to minor, as it becomes the seventh of the IV chord, is important to hear. You'll hear this movement in the next exercise, and even if you simply learn the track by ear, without understanding the theory, you'll internalise this important sound. This movement will be covered in detail in Chapter 6, under "Guide Tones."

ALTERNATING THIRDS AND SEVENTHS 11 13

Slow Blues

Intro (Bass)

THIRD AND SEVENTH OF EACH CHORD [12] [13]

Slow Blues

Intro (Bass)

chorus 1

Bb7	Eb7	Bb7	
3 7	3 7	3 7	7 3
Doo way __	doo yah __	doo way __	doo wah __

Eb7		Bb7	
7 3	3 7	3 7	7 3
doo way __	doo wah __	doo way __	doo wah __

F7	Eb7	Bb7	F7
7 3	3 7	3 7	3 7
doo way __	doo wah __	doo way __	doo wah __

chorus 2

Bb7	Eb7	Bb7	
7 3	7 3	7 3	3 7
Way doo __	wee doo __	way dah __	da way __

Eb7		Bb7	
3 7	7 3	7 3	3 7
way dah __	da way __	way dah ____ yoo	doo way __

F7	Eb7	Bb7	Bb/D Eb6 Edim7	Bb/F F7#5 Bb9
3 7	7 3	7 3		
way dah __	doo way __	way dah ____	ee yah	

Guitar is the quintessential blues instrument. It's so closely connected with blues that it's hard to tell which came first, voices imitating guitars, or guitarists imitating voices. Jeanfrançois Prins plays two choruses of guitar blues licks for you to repeat.

HEAR IT AND SING IT: GUITAR LICKS 14

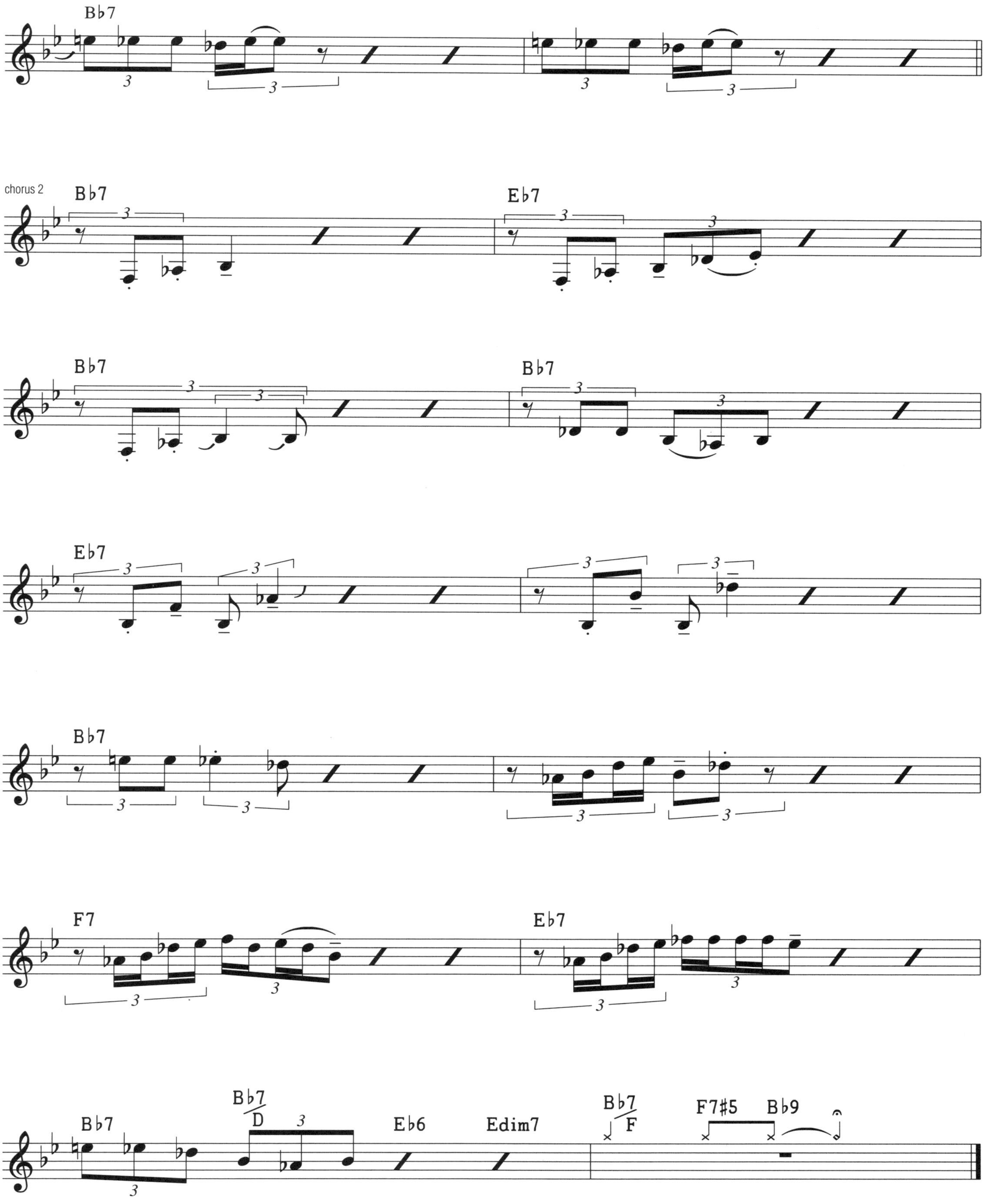
B♭7
chorus 2
B♭7
E♭7
B♭7
B♭7
E♭7
B♭7
F7
E♭7
B♭7
B♭7/D
E♭6
Edim7
B♭7/F
F7♯5
B♭9

Practice suggestions for Basic Blues accompaniment track 4

I am often asked whether I know exactly what notes I'm singing when I improvise. I never think of note names when I am onstage; I just make music. But sometimes I practice with note names and find it useful. The goal is to improvise melodies by ear, and to create an interesting solo. Practicing with note names can help you become conscious of which note you are singing.

- Improvise with the Basic Blues Workout accompaniment track, using the blues scale. Limit yourself to the first note, B♭, and sing the note name. What can you do with one note?

- Experiment with rhythm and dynamics—long tones, staccato, triplets and double time. Remember, rests are also part of music!

- Leap to the same note an octave above or below.

- Then add the next note of the blues scale, D♭, and improvise using only B♭ and D♭, singing the note names

- Continue, adding another note of the scale in each chorus, until you're using the entire blues scale consciously.

- Find a partner who also wants to practice scat singing, and take turns improvising two-measure phrases over the accompaniment-only track. Leave time for your partner to repeat what you've sung. Keep it simple, so that you can sing it again if your partner can't repeat it after hearing it once. This will develop your ear and your musical memory.

- It's useful to practice singing with note names, but after you've mastered the sound of the scale, and you're onstage improvising, connect to the music, listen to your fellow musicians and express yourself!

Scat Syllables

The tradition of scat singing began in the 1920's and has continued evolving up to the present. It began when singers imitated the sounds made by saxophones, trumpets and trombones. Each singer improvised his or her individual scat language. Students often ask which syllables they should use when they improvise. There are no "right" or "wrong" syllables in scat singing; the most important thing is to choose syllables that make the phrasing and dynamics audible. Your choice of syllables can evoke instrumental sounds, express emotions or confound an audience trying to figure out which language you're singing. Be creative, listen to other singers, experiment, and eventually you'll develop your own scat vocabulary.

Listen to a recording of one of your scat solos, and write down a few lines of the syllables you sang. Are you repeating yourself? Which combinations of syllables flow easily? If you notice that you are repeating certain patterns, try adding one new consonant at a time. When I started scatting, I went through the alphabet and tried every consonant and vowel combination I could think of in my morning warm-up. Certain combinations flowed easily for me, and they became part of my scat vocabulary.

The scat syllables you see in this book are transcriptions of improvised solos. It's not necessary for you to sing exactly the same syllables, the important thing is to imitate the rhythmic and musical phrasing. When there is a call and response exercise, your role is to answer, repeating the phrase. Keep the rhythmic value of the notes, but feel free to use syllables that feel natural to you.

You'll notice that consonant pairs like "bw," "vw" and "dw" are often used to slide into a note ("bwee," "vway," "dwop"). Often "ow" ("dow," "bow," "wow") indicates a "fall-off," where the pitch drops down at the end of the note. Be aware of the endings of notes; rests are also part of the music, and where you end a note can add to or subtract from the overall groove. In written scat solos, the "plosive" consonants at the end of a syllable ("p," "t" and "k"), are not released, but held back, in what is called a "stop articulation." For example, at the end of "doot," the tongue remains on the roof of the mouth, stopping the tone without the sound of released air normally heard on a final "t." With the final "p," as in "dop," the lips simply close without an audible release of air.

DEVELOPING YOUR OWN SCAT VOCABULARY

- Build your vocabulary by experimenting with different vowel and consonant combinations.

- Beginners should start with the consonants, "b" and "d" and the vowels "ah," "oo" and "ee." Using these vowels will help you create a consistent sound, and the consonants, which avoid plosives and glottal articulation, will allow your melodies to flow smoothly.

- For flexibility and speed, try alternating "d" and "b" as beginning consonants ("da-ba-da-ba," "deh-beh-deh-beh," etc.).

- For triplets "doo-dle-a," "did-lee-a," "dih-lee-a," "dah-ee-a" or "doo-ee-a" flow easily.

- Use various consonants and vowel combinations. For a systematic approach, start with "d," "b" and "v," combined with the five basic English vowel sounds "ah," "ay," "ee," "oh" and "oo."

- Using clear vowel sounds will improve your intonation.

- After you feel comfortable with those sounds, add new consonants one at a time: "l," "s," "sh," "v," etc., as well as other vowel sounds. Practice different combinations.

- Scat syllables should roll off the tongue. Practice them in order to become fluent with your new vocabulary.

- Practice singing up-tempo passages with a metronome. Start at 60 beats per minute, and increase your speed by one notch each day.

- Syllables evoke certain eras of jazz: "Vo dee oh do" sounds like the 1920s, "Shu lee a bop" brings the 1940s to mind, "La la leh oh" sounds good on African grooves, "Vah veh vo" works well for Brazilian tunes.

Pronunciation Guide for Scat Syllables

When you see this written in this book:	The International Phonetic Association (IPA) abbreviation is:	Here is an English language example:
ee	i	b<u>ee</u>
eh	ɛ	b<u>e</u>d
ay	e (or eɪ)	p<u>ay</u>
o	əʊ	n<u>o</u>
oo	u	b<u>oo</u>t
a	ɑ	f<u>a</u>ther
ah	ɑ:	as in f<u>a</u>ther (but held longer)
o followed by a consonant other than h	ɑ	sh<u>o</u>p
aw	ɔ	<u>aw</u>e
a followed by a consonant other than h	æ	sc<u>a</u>t
uh	ʌ	b<u>u</u>t
i	ɪ	s<u>i</u>t
ai	ɑɪ	p<u>ie</u>
ow	aʊ	<u>ou</u>t
u followed by a consonant other than h	ʊ	b<u>oo</u>k
yoo	ju	you

Chapter 3: Blues Riffs and Riff Blues

A "blues riff" is a short musical phrase based on the blues scale. To "riff" is to repeat a phrase throughout a chorus, usually as an accompaniment for a soloist in a big band or ensemble. Riffing creates a background that's a musical springboard for the soloist, lifting him up to a higher energy level. Many well-known big band and jazz blues are made up entirely of riffs, or "riff blues." (See the appendix for a list of riff blues.)

Since You've Gone is a 12-measure blues, based on a riff that is repeated three times. The chord progression is slightly more complex than that of the Basic Blues. It uses the **IV7** chord in the second and tenth measures (shown in parentheses in the chart on page 11). However, when you improvise, you can still sing the pentatonic or blues scale over the whole song, as I've illustrated in the "hear it and sing it" section.

The first two choruses are in the traditional blues lyric form: **A - A - B**. The next two choruses are "stop time," meaning that the band plays "hits" on the first beat of each of the first four measures. Many traditional blues have stop time choruses. When you ask for stop time on a blues at a jam session, it provides space for you to stand out for a moment and adds a new element to the arrangement. After the stop time choruses on *Since You've Gone*, you'll hear two choruses of two-measure phrases for you to repeat. These phrases are built on the blues scale, to help you become more comfortable using it in scat singing.

As you work on this song, you'll have a chance to apply what you've learned about scales and scat syllables. You'll also have the opportunity to expand your scat syllable vocabulary by learning improvised solos sung by two of the foremost male jazz singers on the scene.

vocal lead sheet
B♭

Since You've Gone 15 19

Judy Niemack

Medium swing

It's so strange, you act like someone I never knew. I had to call my doctor, I lost my appetite. The things I told her shocked her, she told me I should fight and I would but love keeps lead-in' me on. If I could I'd pack the things I've got and be gone.

Soo ba doo blay-ee yo bee dee ya

Sa ba ba ba ba ba doo bay bay doot ba ba ba bay da doo bow

see ya yo yee yo ba dee ya

hear it and sing it chorus 2
B♭7 even 8ths
E♭7
B♭7
Fm7 B♭7
Sa ya ya ya doo . ba doo dee doo dot dat day yoo da
E♭7 laid back
Edim7
B♭7/F
G7
Sho vay vah voh va voo vay vee vee vee vee vee ah
Cm7
F7
B♭7 D♭7
Cm7 F7
Sho vwee va ooh va ooh voo vweep vay ow
If I ev-
out melody
B♭7
E♭7
B♭7
- er hear my ba - by call - in' my name,
if I ev-
E♭7
B♭7
- er hear my ba - by call - in' my name,
I'll be there
B♭7
E♭7
B♭7(♯9)/D E♭7 Edim7
B♭7/D B7 B9
B♭9(♯11)
as sure as sun-shine fol-lows the rain.
Oh yeah yeah

Chapter 3: Blues Riffs and Riff Blues

Now that the blues form and harmonies are familiar to you, it's easier to improvise over them. If you're wondering where to begin, just start with the melody, substituting syllables for the lyrics, and see where that takes you. Here's an example—I've transcribed my syllables for you, but feel free to experiment with your own.

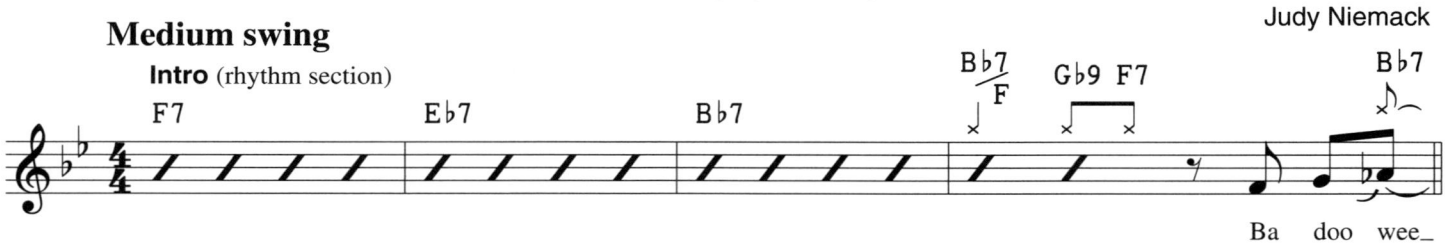

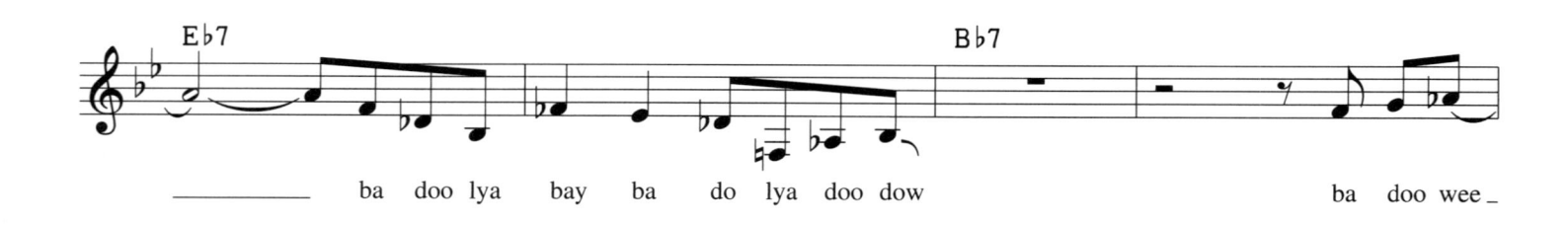

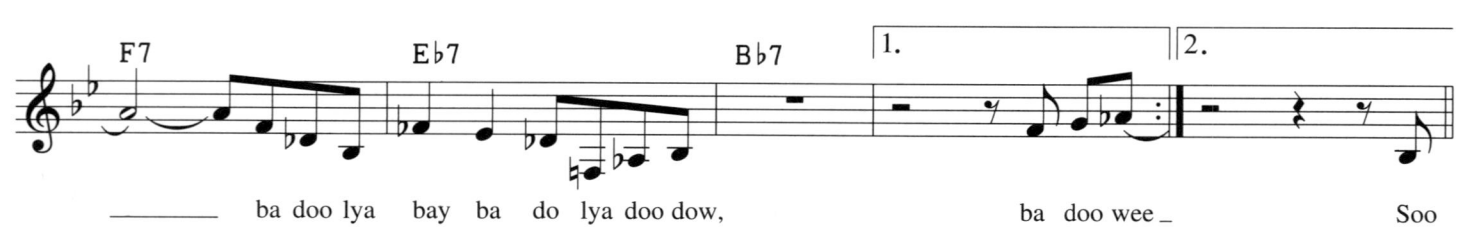

transcription
B♭

SINCE YOU'VE GONE

Scat Version (Judy Niemack)

Judy Niemack

Medium swing

Copyright © 2011 Second Floor Music

Judy Niemack's *Hear It and Sing It! Exploring the Blues* Chapter 3: Blues Riffs and Riff Blues   35

stop time chorus 1

B♭7

Vlay vlay dool yoo dah ow __ sav - voo an dow see n doh do-ay

dee ya da n dah

E♭7

bo way ba da bee ba-o doo way

B♭7

sa da ba da vlee bee - ee ya dow __

F7

va va vwee va dee ya va

E♭7

dee ya vay __ dee dow __

B♭7

F7

su vla

stop time chorus 2

B♭7

vlayt dit day ya dool ya dayt sa dah __ doo yoo vay vo wa va dwi va

doot sa ya doo doo wee __

E♭7

ba da boo bwe - e dee ah __

B♭7

ah ow __

F7

va doo vlay __ doo da doo ya do n

day __ day __ dow day dow __

fade out

Listen to Mark Murphy scatting *Since You've Gone*. After singing the melody, he improvises over the stop time choruses. Then he sings two choruses of phrases for you to repeat. Try imitating Mark's scat syllables; he has a unique vocabulary of sounds which were a challenge to transcribe.

Mark Murphy is one of the top jazz vocalists performing today. He captivates crowds with his soulful voice, a unique style and an immediately identifiable sound. Composer Alec Wilder said, "Mark's musicianship, range, intonation, diction, inventiveness and incredible rhythmic sense are all of a piece and all marvelous." Ella Fitzgerald declared, "He is my equal."

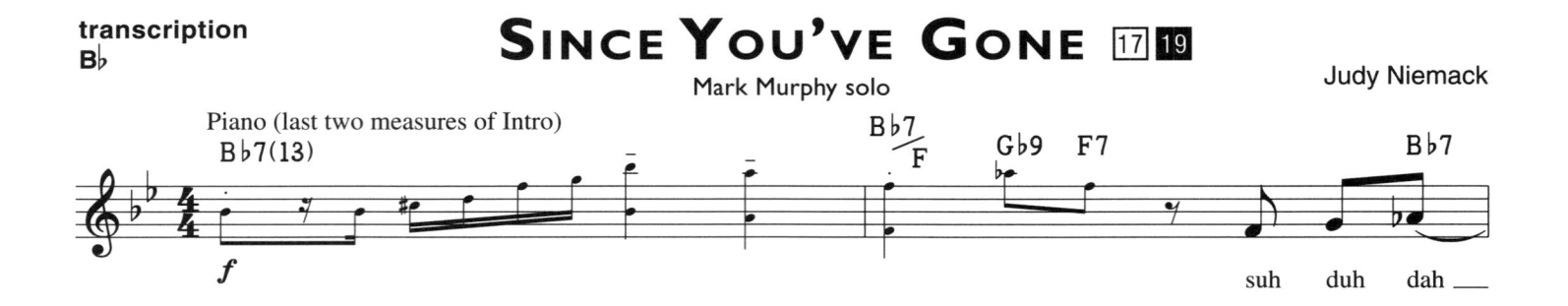

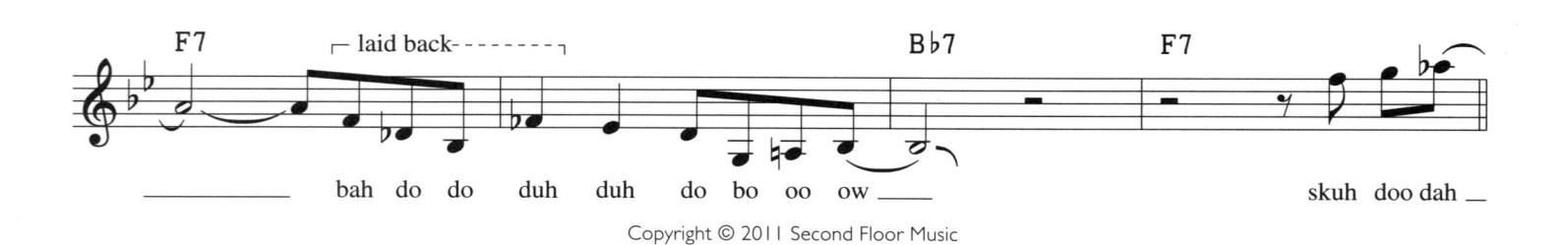

transcription
Bb

Since You've Gone

Mark Murphy solo

Judy Niemack

Copyright © 2011 Second Floor Music

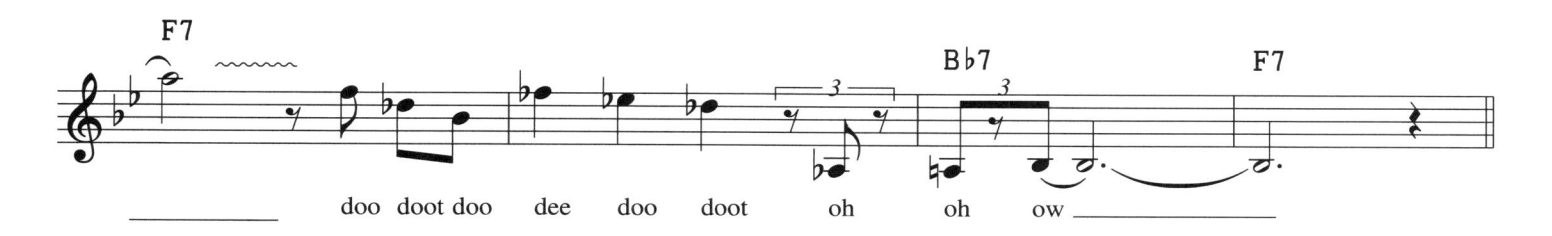

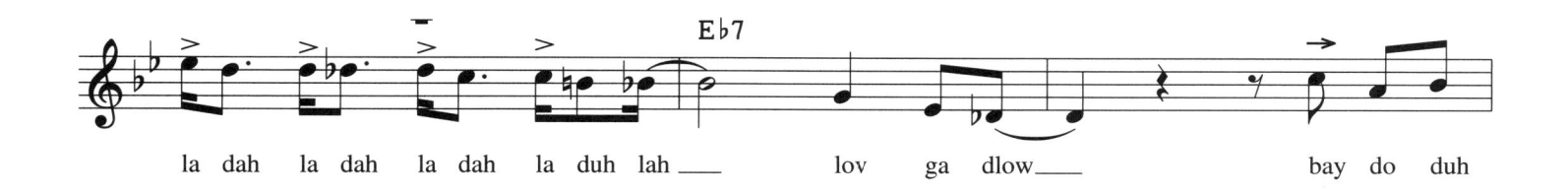

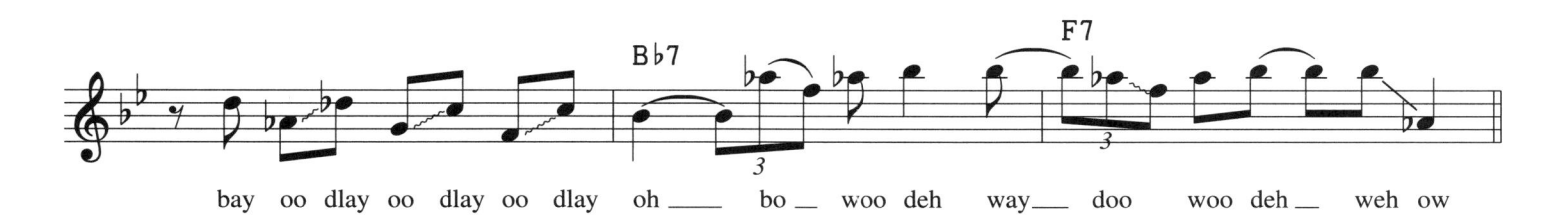

Judy Niemack's *Hear It and Sing It! Exploring the Blues* Chapter 3: Blues Riffs and Riff Blues 37

melody chorus 2

_____ boo doo doo bee doo doo o wuh duh day dow   skuh doo dah___

_____ bah do n eh uh duh b doo ah _____   skoo deh dow___

_____ doo doot doo dee doo doot oh oh ow _____

stop time chorus 1

sal lul lul lul day uh da n doo dut   va oo dle a vay dah la dah

la dah la dah la dah la duh lah ___   lov ga dlow ___   bay do duh

blay da vo do d buh day wuh day wow___ bo dle lay dl dlay___ oo day oo duh bl do___ doodle ay

bay oo dlay oo dlay oo dlay oh ___ bo___ woo deh way___ doo woo deh___ weh ow

38 Chapter 3: Blues Riffs and Riff Blues

stop time chorus 2

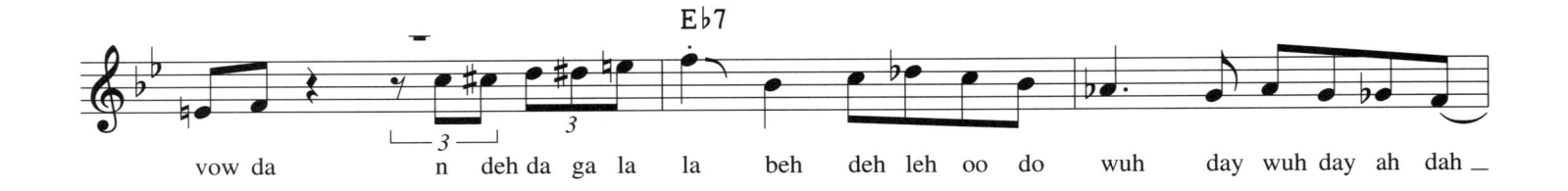

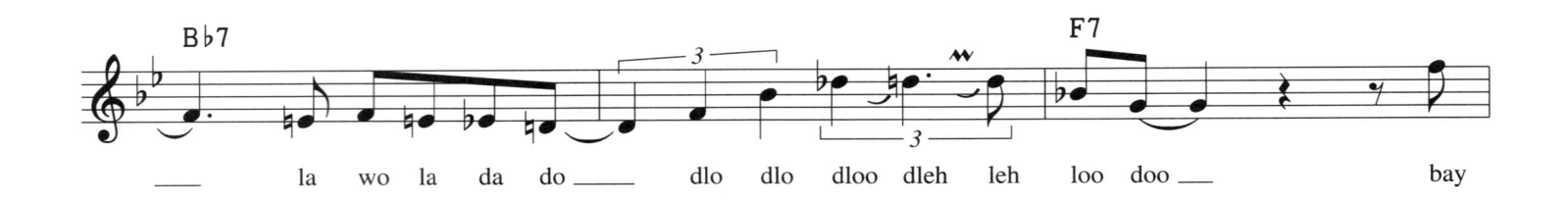

Bb7 | Eb7 | Bb7 |

bee doo ga oo day oo day doo doop boo boo boo wah day doo dn deh

Eb7

vow da n deh da ga la la beh deh leh oo do wuh day wuh day ah dah

Bb7 | F7

la wo la da do dlo dlo dloo dleh leh loo doo bay

Bb7 | F7

eh duh oo dle doo dle oo dey doo doo deh doo doo eh deh deh oo deh deh oo oo deh deh

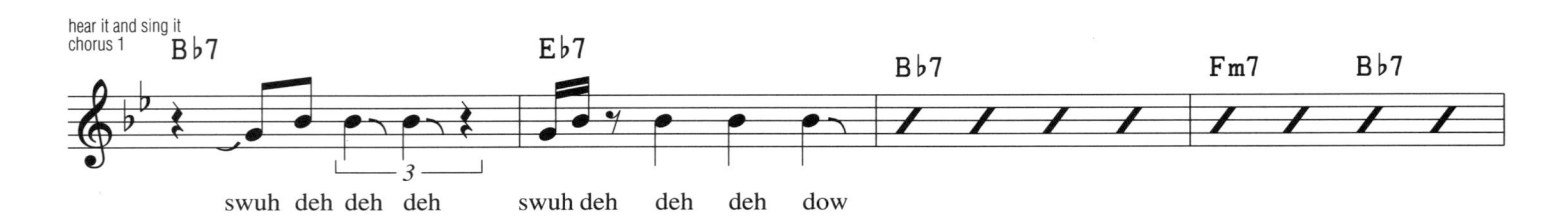

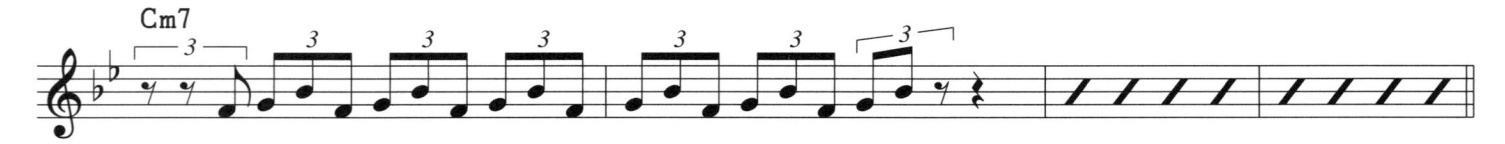

hear it and sing it chorus 1

Bb7 | Eb7 | Bb7 | Fm7 | Bb7

swuh deh deh deh swuh deh deh deh dow

Eb7 | Edim7 | Bb7/F | G7
— double time feel ————————————

bay uh duh do deh duh do bay uh duh do dey yuh do

Cm7

oo loo deh dl oo deh dl oo deh dl oo deh dl oo deh dl oo deh

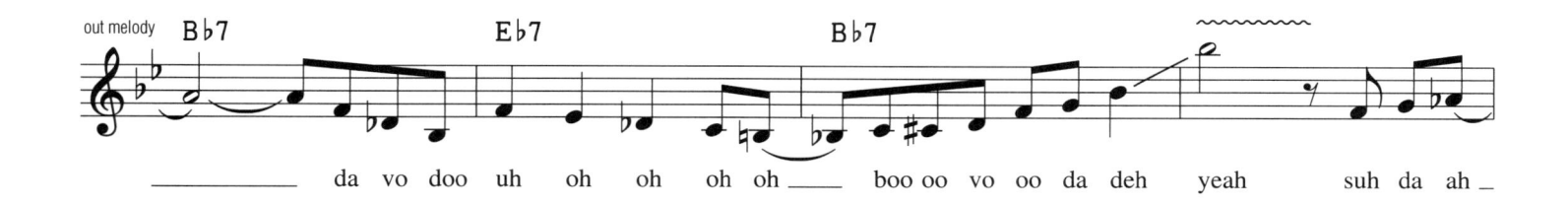

Judy Niemack's *Hear It and Sing It! Exploring the Blues* — Chapter 3: Blues Riffs and Riff Blues

Chapter 3: Blues Riffs and Riff Blues

I asked Darmon Meader to jam with me on *Since You've Gone*. I've transcribed Darmon's scat solo on the stop time choruses as well as two choruses where we "traded twos" (exchanged two-bar phrases). As musicians sharing a common jazz language, we naturally react to and expand upon each other's ideas. In an improvised duo, the challenge is to listen to the other person while creating your own melody. Listen to Darmon singing an inner call and response on the final melody chorus.

Recognized in both the vocal and instrumental jazz scenes, Darmon Meader has achieved international renown as the founder, musical director, chief arranger, composer, producer, saxophonist and vocalist with The New York Voices.

transcription
B♭

SINCE YOU'VE GONE

Darmon Meader and Judy Niemack jamming

Judy Niemack

Copyright © 2011 Second Floor Music

F7 Eb7
doot n voo eh soo doop voo da voo va voo va dee day
Bb7 F7
voo vip vi doo m bi doo n vo voo wee ay
Judy
stop time chorus 2
Sa yad - da yad - dli duh doot dee deet ba day doo bo bay n doo buh
Eb7
m bo beh m bo boo boo bweep doo doo ba day n da yow sa
Bb7 G7 Cm7
dap dla dla sa da ba vo vay vwee voo ooee ya dot dlay day oh so
F7 Bb7 F7
Darmon
dlay dlay dlo dlay dlo dla loo vo vway oh vay ah ow soo bay

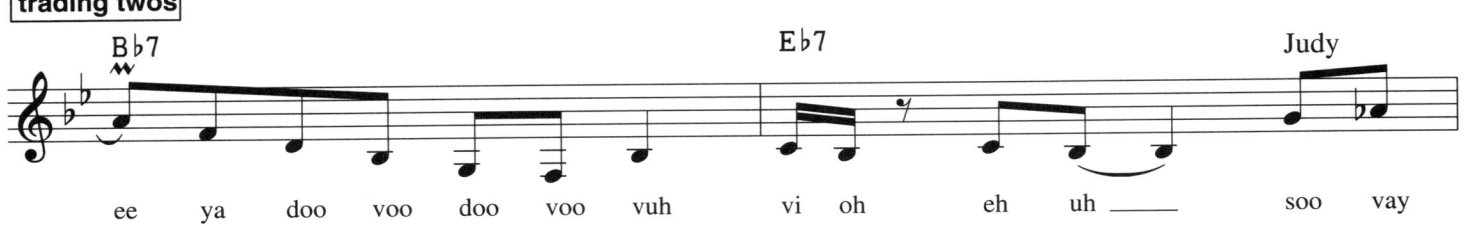

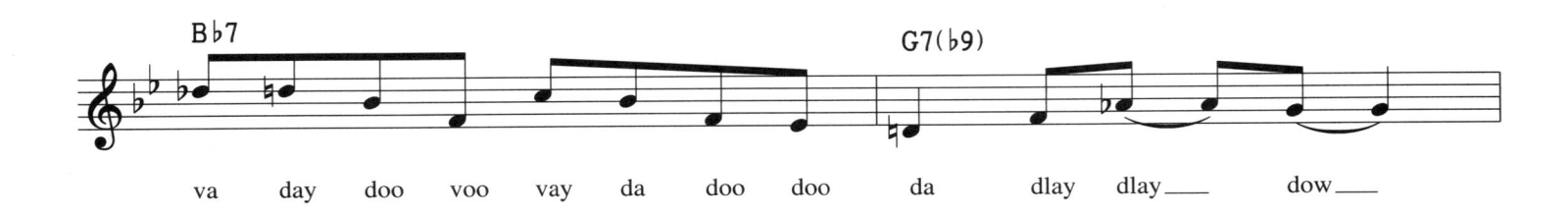

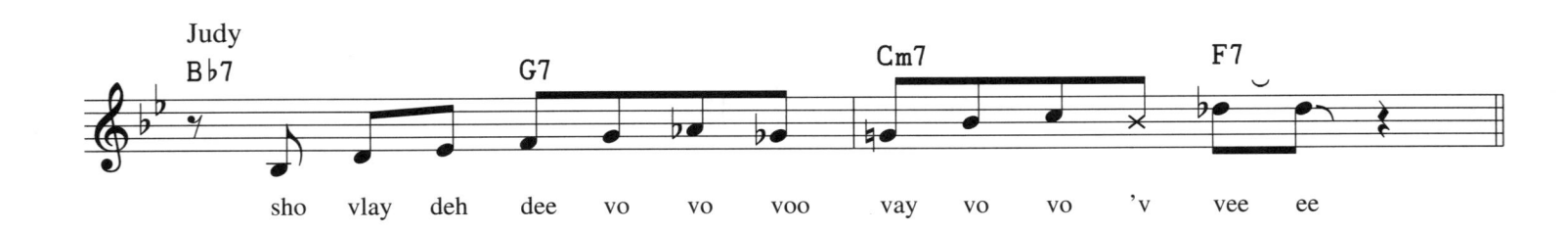

Chapter 3: Blues Riffs and Riff Blues

trading twos

Bb7 … Eb7 … Judy
ee ya doo voo doo voo vuh — vi oh eh uh ___ soo vay

Bb7 … Darmon
di lya do veh dee yuh va vo — vee va va voo vwee sa

Eb7 … Edim7 … Judy
voo vo voo vo voo vo voo vo — voo voo vo vo vah soo

Bb7 … G7(b9)
va day doo voo vay da doo doo — da dlay dlay___ dow___

Darmon
Cm7 … F7
sih vi voo voo vo voo veh voo — vo vo vo va vuh ee yay___

Judy
Bb7 … G7 … Cm7 … F7
sho vlay deh dee vo vo voo — vay vo vo 'v vee ee

Darmon
B♭7
seh yeht seh yeh
E♭7
seh yeht seh yeh
Judy
B♭7
see ee say ay say yay say ay
Darmon
say yay
E♭7
say ay say ay soo va doo vay voo
Edim7
vay voo way
Judy
sho va do va
B♭7
dip dip doop doop bwi buh do va
G7
sweev va voo voo vo
Darmon
sah
Cm7
va voo va o vo voo va
F7
o va doo way
Judy
sa
B♭7
vlay va doot n day a dn
Cm7
dai yoo
F7
dow
Judy
out melody
B♭7
vee va dool yoo
E♭7
vayp vap va ya ah ow
B♭7
Darmon
voo doo way
laid back
see duh va vo va vuh vuh

44 Chapter 3: Blues Riffs and Riff Blues

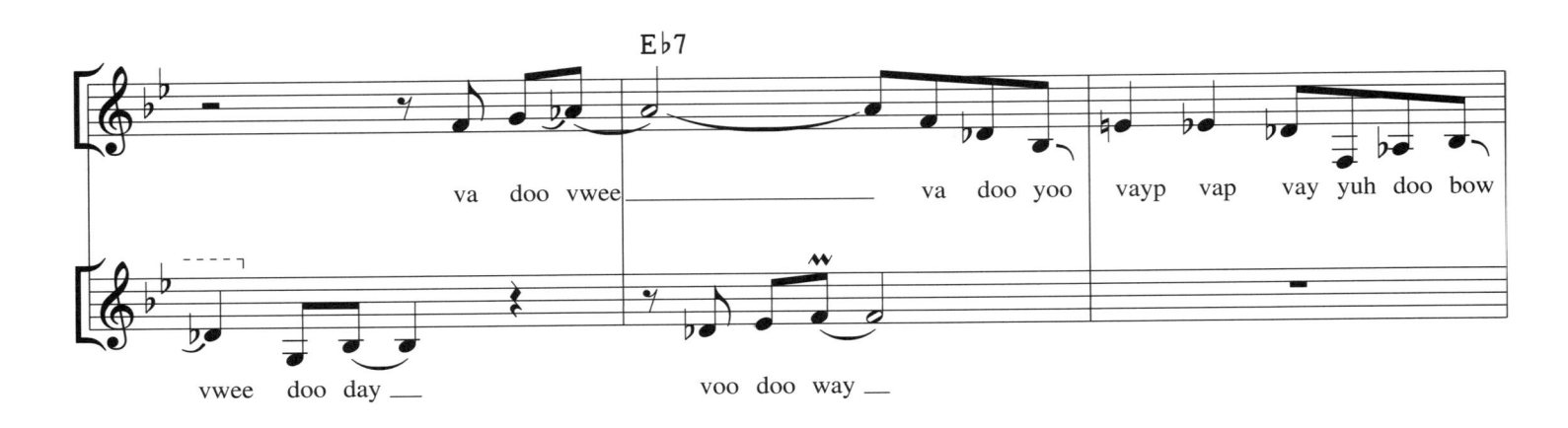

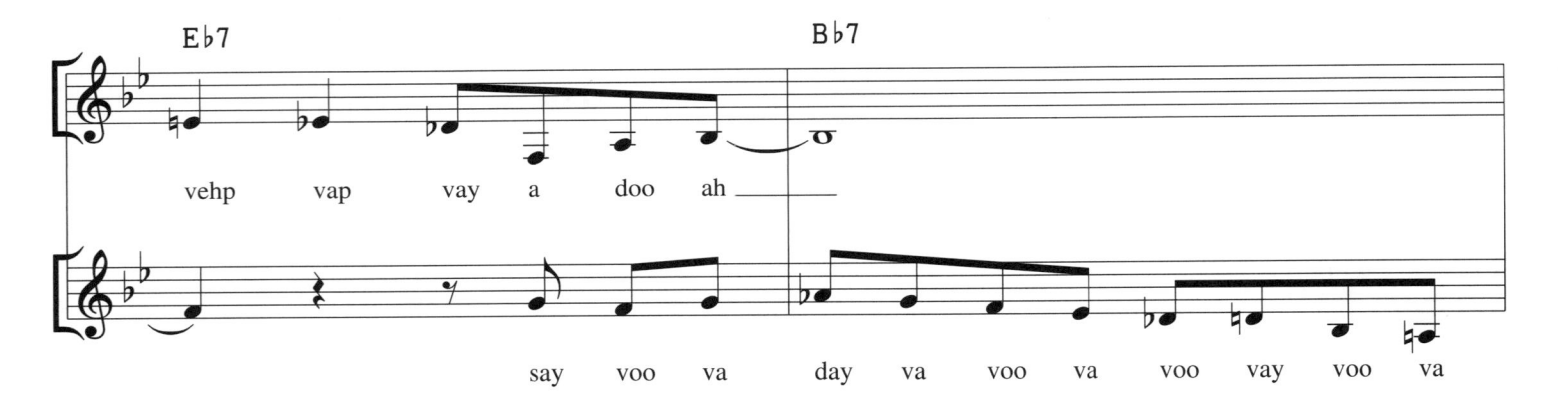

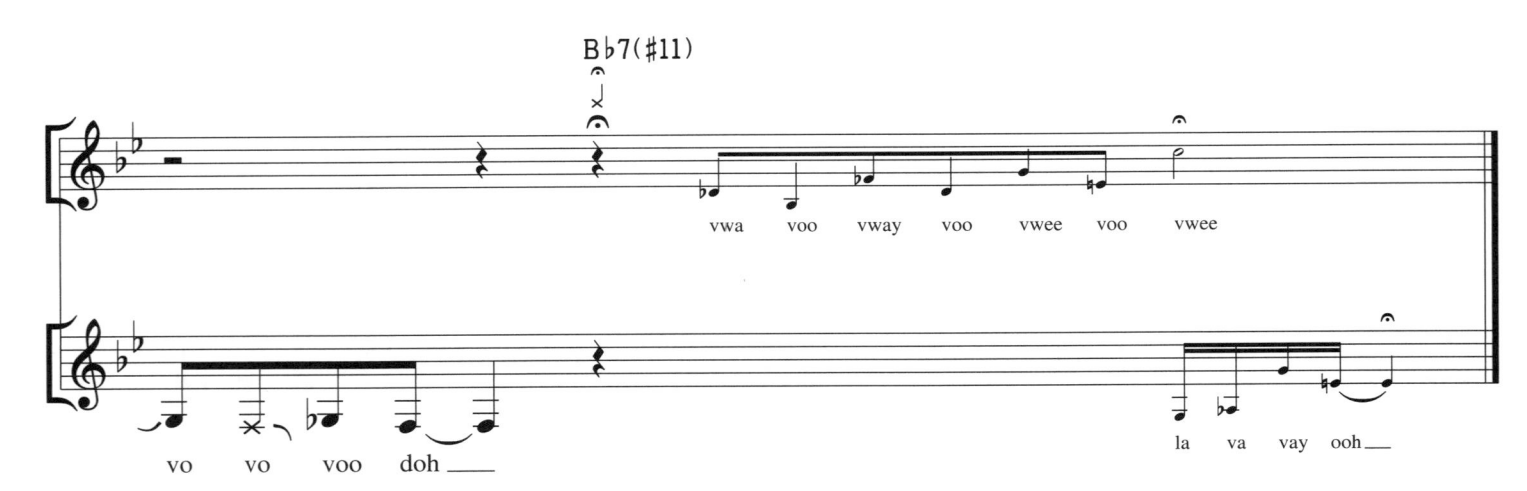

CHAPTER 4: MINOR BLUES

Minor blues follow the same basic harmonic motion as major blues. Lower case letters indicate minor chords.

tonic (i) sometimes with subdominant in bar two
subdominant (iv) sometimes back to tonic
dominant (V) sometimes via subdominant back to tonic

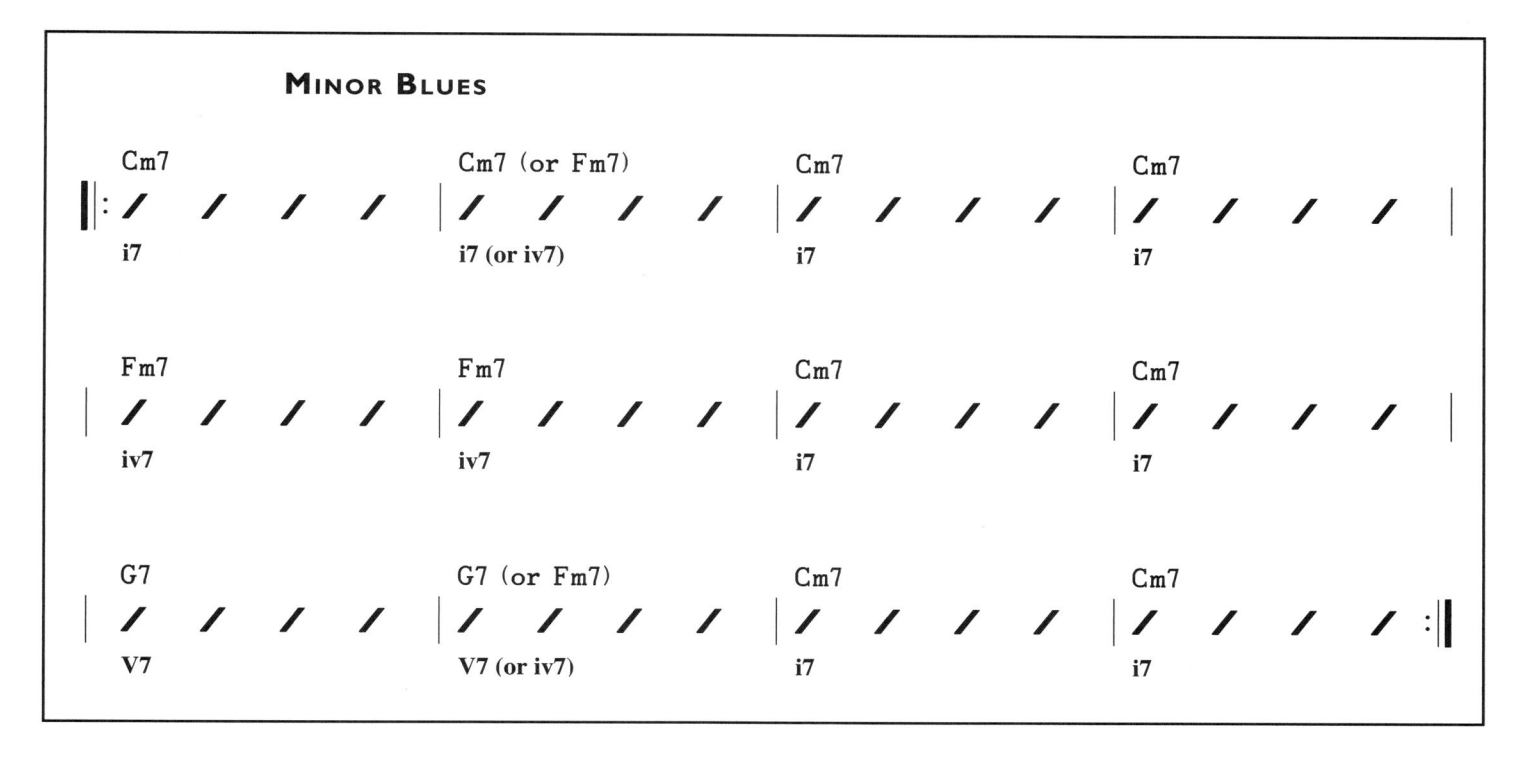

MINOR BLUES

Cm7	Cm7 (or Fm7)	Cm7	Cm7
i7	i7 (or iv7)	i7	i7
Fm7	Fm7	Cm7	Cm7
iv7	iv7	i7	i7
G7	G7 (or Fm7)	Cm7	Cm7
V7	V7 (or iv7)	i7	i7

However, it is common to have a slightly different chord progression in measures 9 and 10, a chromatic approach to the **V** chord, also known as a "tritone substitution." *Something to Say* is an example of this type of minor blues form. The lead sheet is on the next page, and page 48 has a transcription of a minor blues solo with an analysis of the solo.

Here are some of my favorite minor blues songs:

Ancient Footprints (Wayne Shorter, Kitty Margolis) (Instrumentally known as *Footprints*)
Comin' Home Baby (Bob Dorough, Ben Tucker)
Goodbye Pork Pie Hat (Charles Mingus, Joni Mitchell)
Interplay (Bill Evans, Judy Niemack)
Mr. P.C. (John Coltrane, Jon Hendricks)
Señor Blues (Horace Silver)
Stolen Moments (Oliver Nelson, Mark Murphy)

46 Chapter 4: Minor Blues

Something To Say

vocal lead sheet
Cm

Judy Niemack

Medium swing

melody chorus 1

There's some-thing that I've got to say and it's the rea-son I've been cry-in'. There's some-thing that I've got to say and it's the rea-son I've been cry-in'. I could-n't wait an-oth-er day, our love is dy-in'. Well, I've been feel-in' pret-ty bad, the oth-er day I caught you ly-in'.

melody chorus 2

Well, I've been feel-in' pret-ty bad, the oth-er day I caught you ly-in'. You know it makes me real-ly sad you just stopped try-in'. If you just want to run a-

Copyright © 2011 Second Floor Music

melody chorus 3
Cm7
round, don't both - er com - in' back to my place.
Fm7
even 8ths
If you just want to run a - round, don't both-er com-in' back to
Cm7
3
Ab7
my place, 'cause there is some-thin' I have fou - nd:
G7
Cm7
Dm7b5
G7
I won't miss your face. So pack your bags, you got - ta go
melody chorus 4
Cm7
and set me free to face to - mor -
Fm7
- row. So pack your bags and go and set me free to face to -
Cm7
Ab7
mor - row. And I'll be strong a - gain, I know,
G7
Cm7
Bbm7
Eb7
af - ter this sor - row. And I'll be strong
Abmaj7
G7
3
Cm7
a - gain, I know, af - ter this sor - row.

MINOR BLUES SOLO ON SOMETHING TO SAY [21]

Chorus 1

- As Plato said, "The beginning is the most important part of the work." When you begin your solo with a simple melodic statement, you have somewhere to go. Stay with your first idea and develop it through repetition, sequences or rhythmic variation until you're ready to move on. Your solo will unfold and lead you naturally to the next motif, or musical idea.

transcription
Cm

[Musical notation with lyrics:]

Sha va day dwee ow

sa va day dwee dow

va da va vlay dlay dloh sha da va vo vay ay a daw

su dut vee-ee-ooh bee ah

Chorus 2

- If you're going to continue your solo for a second chorus, don't let the energy sag at the end of the first chorus. Direct your melodic line towards a point in the following chorus. For example, at the end of Chorus 1, in bars 10, 11 and 12, you'll see a repeated three-note interval pattern that crosses the bar line and leads into the next chorus. This technique also works well at jam sessions, where you need to make it clear that you're going to take another chorus, so that the next soloist doesn't begin to play.

Judy Niemack's *Hear It and Sing It! Exploring the Blues* — Chapter 4: Minor Blues

chorus 2

_ zay doo dlay doo-dle o vay dil ya do sa vay dut do vay
dul ya do vay ay a dwee yah sho va va vay doo
da dan dop vee ah ___ say da dow ba bwee ba boo yoo
di - n suh-dle li-dle lo beh day yo beh day sha vla day da day va vo do

Chorus 3

- Add rhythmic interest with double-time phrases or triplets.

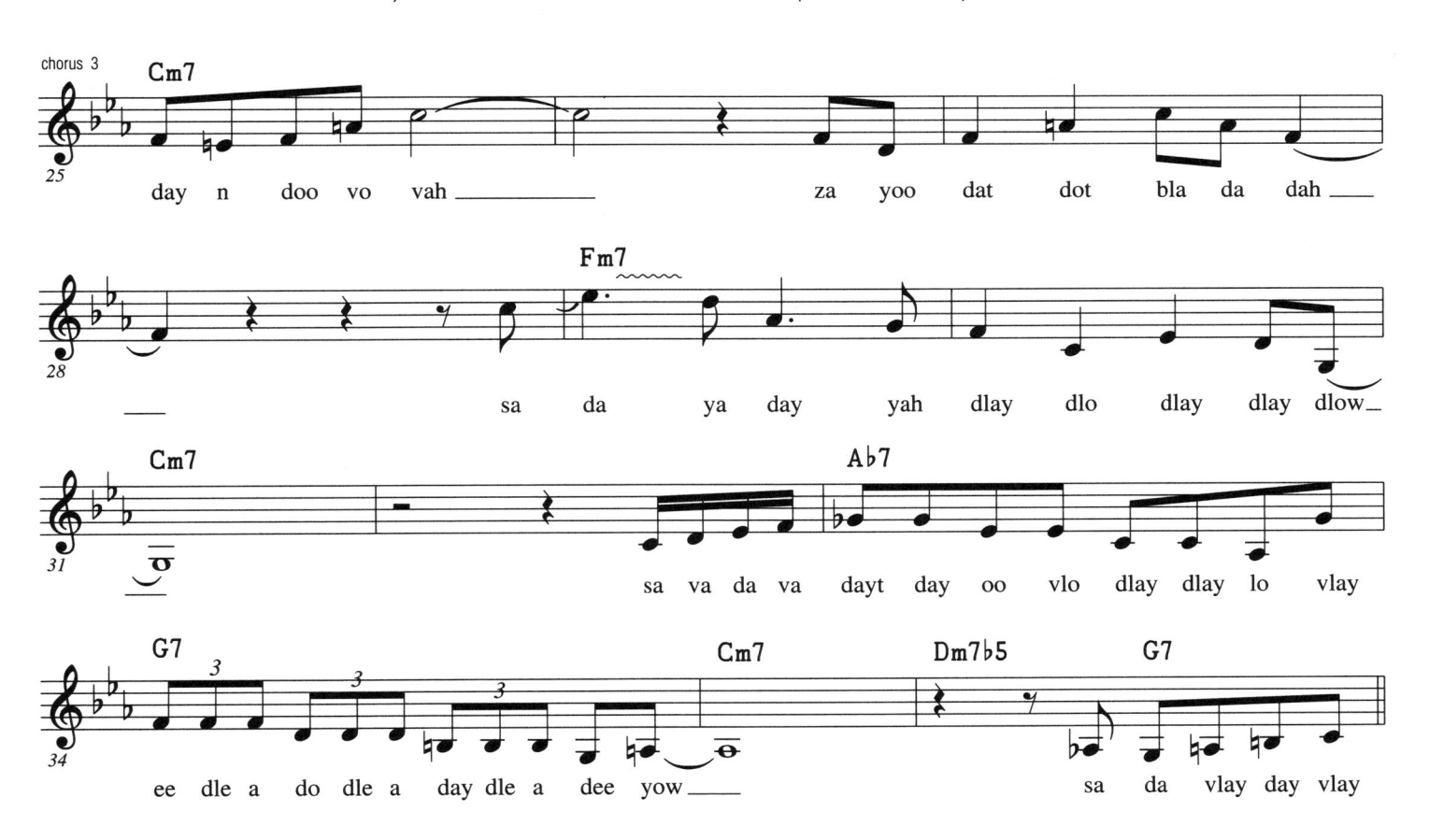

chorus 3

day n doo vo vah ___ za yoo dat dot bla da dah ___
sa da ya day yah dlay dlo dlay dlay dlow ___
sa va da va dayt day oo vlo dlay dlay lo vlay
ee dle a do dle a day dle a dee yow ___ sa da vlay day vlay

Chorus 4

- Here is another example of a phrase that crosses the last measure of chorus 3, continuing into the first measure of chorus 4. The ascending four-note motif is sung twice using eighth notes, then repeated using triplets, causing the acccents to fall on different notes of the motif. This is called "rhythmic displacement" and is an interesting way to vary a melody.
- In measures 41-42, I used the blues scale, ending on the sixth degree of the C dorian scale, a more modern sound.
- In measure 46 the root of the chord (G) is approached chromatically from above, which increases the release of tension felt when we land on the tonic of a chord.
- The final note is the fourth degree of the C dorian minor scale, which gives it an unresolved quality common in a jazz blues.

On the next page is a minor blues composed by "The Little Giant," tenor saxophonist Johnny Griffin. Jazz drummer Philly Joe Jones recorded Griffin's *Blues For Dracula* at a session at Rudy Van Gelder's studio in 1958, and he improvised a hilarious Count Dracula impression over the introduction. Inspired by that recording and a visit to Romania, where I visited Transylvania and saw Bran Castle, the home of the infamous Count, I wrote these lyrics. Sheila Jordan joined me, improvising a solo in a spooky mood.

Sheila Jordan is an icon of vocal jazz and has been inspiring generations of singers with her intimate and inventive style since the release of her Blue Note album, "Portrait of Sheila," in 1962. One of the first artists to teach vocal jazz at the college level, she encourages younger singers to develop their own style and to "be real." Sheila continues to teach and tour, performing worldwide. She recorded this session at the age of eighty.

On this track, Sheila holds the attention of the listener for four choruses by telling a story, alternating scat with improvised lyrics, using repeated motifs and varying dynamics. She starts with a blues scale, then answers herself, leaving a pause between. Her phrases sound almost like spoken sentences; each one has a clear beginning and ending. She improvises rhymed lyrics about "that dirty bat" and "that Dracula cat." She quotes Dizzy Gillespie's famous song, *Ool-ya-koo,* then moves fluidly between scat and lyrics in the third chorus with a phrase, repeated several times, which becomes "Here he comes, here he comes, here he comes...." In the last chorus, she sings a melody of descending thirds, repeats it with variations, then advises quietly: "Watch your jugular vein, 'cause this cat's insane!" and ends with a loud, high note on "There he goes...."

Try these techniques when you sing with the accompaniment-only track:
- Focus on telling a story, whether singing lyrics or using scat syllables.
- Give each phrase a clear beginning and ending.
- Alternate improvising lyrics with scatting.
- Use repeated musical motifs to bridge scat and lyrics.
- Vary your dynamics.

The Count Is Back

Instrumentally known as "Blues For Dracula"

vocal lead sheet
A♭m

Music by Johnny Griffin
Lyric by Judy Niemack

Slow swing (♩ = ca. 68)

Lyrics:

The Count is back, he's hang-in' 'round. He needs a snack, you hear a sound. The moon is high, the air is still, he pass-es by, you feel a chill. When he comes in through your win-dow, all dressed in black, there's no way back. He's look-in'

glum, he wants his bride. You'd bet-ter run, you'd bet-ter hide. The sun is down, don't stick a-round, un-less you're on some sac-red ground. When he comes in through your win-dow, he wants to drain your jug-'lar

Copyright © 1958 (renewed 1986), 2011 Second Floor Music

Judy Niemack's Hear It and Sing It! Exploring the Blues — Chapter 4: Minor Blues — 53

2. to solos
Ab Eb Ab Ab7(#9)
vein.

Solos 4 Sheila Jordan solo choruses
Abm | Bbm7b5 Eb7 | Abm
4-feel

Ebm7 Ab7 | Dbm /Cb | Bbm7b5 Eb7

Abm /Gb | F7 | E7

Eb7 | Abm | Eb7 :|| Eb7
1.,2.,3.   **4. last time**
He's look-in'

out melody
Ab Eb Ab Ab7(#9) | Ab Eb Ab Ab7(#9)
glum,   he wants his bride.   You'd bet-ter
back,   he's hang-in' 'round. He needs a

Ab Eb Ab Ab7(#9) | Ab Eb Ab Ab7(#9)
run,   you'd bet-ter hide.   The sun is
snack,   you hear a sound.   The moon is

Db Ab Db Db7(#9) | Db Ab Db Db7(#9) | Ab Eb Ab Ab7(#9)
down,   don't stick a-round, unless you live   on sac-red
high,   the air is still,   he pass-es by,   you feel a

54 Chapter 4: Minor Blues

Lyrics (verse 1 / verse 2):

ground. When he comes in through your win-dow, he wants to drain your jug-'lar vein. The Count is back.

chill. When he comes in through your win-dow, all dressed in black, there's no way

That ma-ni-ac, he will at-tack. He's see-ing red, 'cause he's un-dead. That dap-per stud, he's out for blood. He'll bite your throat, and then he'll gloat. One fi-nal note, that's all she wrote.

Jazz musicians sometimes alternate improvising solos in two-, four- or eight-measure phrases with each other after they've taken their solos. It's called "trading twos," "trading fours," etc. Try answering Sheila's twos with your own improvisations.

transcription
A♭m

TRADING TWOS WITH SHEILA JORDAN 🔲 24

Dbm /Cb Bbm7b5 Eb7
doo-dle eh day doo-dle eh day doo-dle eh day doo-dle eh day doo-dle eh deht deft day dut dut doi
Abm /Gb F7
ho - uh
E7 Eb7
did n dli di-dle dli di-dle-i-di di-dle-i di-dle-i di-dle-i deh
Abm Eb7
the
chorus 3
Abm Bbm7b5 Eb7
bat the bad bat the bad bat the bad bat the bad bat the bad bat the bad
Abm Ebm7 Ab7
bat
Dbm /Cb Bbm7b5 Eb7
scat scat scat scat scat scat scat scat scat scat
Abm /Gb F7

Judy Niemack's *Hear It and Sing It! Exploring the Blues* — Chapter 4: Minor Blues

chorus 4

Lyrics under the staves:

wi pih wih pih di di di di di di deh deh deh deh deh deh di di day

lo deh deh ___ lo do deh deh lo lo deh deh lo do de heh deh deh deh

day

dil ya dil ya dil ya dil ya dil dle a did le a dee hip boo ba deh deh ___

bo weh ___ doo leh ___ doo leh de deh de doo lah deh deh de doo le de deh de deh eh deh eh ___

Chapter 5: Jazz Blues

Blues music was a major influence in the development of jazz. Jazz musicians, searching for new ways to play blues, modified and altered the basic chord progression. They added chords and harmonic extensions of the chords, and later even chord substitutions. (To create a "chord substitution," a chord in the original progression is replaced by one or more chords that have the same general "sense" or function, but add a different color or a secondary harmonic movement.) A jazz blues will usually have a more sophisticated treatment of the harmony than a traditional blues would. Jazz musicians have written blues waltzes (Toots Thielemans' *Bluesette*), blues marches (Benny Golson's *Blues March*) and blues with substitute chord changes (Charles Mingus's *Goodbye Pork Pie Hat*). These and many other variations descended from the original three-chord blues.

On the opposite page are five common blues progressions used in jazz, in order of complexity, all shown in the key of C. Play each one slowly on the piano, or ask an accompanist to play them for you. Spot the differences in each one, and compare how they sound.

On page 61, you'll find a method that can be applied to learning these chord progressions, based on the jazz blues, *New Concept (For a Blue Planet)*. We'll explore this song in depth, singing the changes and learning to improvise with the *Jazz Blues Workout*.

Five Common Jazz Blues Progressions

1.
| C7 | F7 | C7 | C7 | F7 | F7 | C7 | A7 | Dm7 | G7 | C7 | Dm7 G7 |

2.
| C7 | F7 | C7 | Gm7 C7 | F7 | F#dim7 | C7/G | A7 | Dm7 | G7 | Em7 A7 | Dm7 G7 |

3.
| C7 | Bb7 | Ab7 | Gb7 | F7 | F#dim7 | C7/G | A7 | D7 | G7 | C7 A7 | D7 G7 |

4.
| C7 | F7 | C7 Db7 | C7 | F7 | F7 | Cmaj7 Dm7 | Em7 Ebm7 Dm7 | Dbmaj7 | C7 | F7 | C7 G7 |

5. "Stormy Monday Blues"
| C7 | F7 | C7 | Gm7 C7 | F7 | F#m7 B7 | C7 | Em7 A7 | Dm7 G7 | Abm7 Db7 | C7 | Eb7 Ab7 Db7 |

Singing the changes

In addition to using the blues or pentatonic scale in soloing, you can also use the specific scales that go with each different chord in a blues progression. Accomplished jazz improvisers can easily move between blues, pentatonic and the various scales implied by the chord progression.

As vocalists, we don't have keys to play, buttons to press or strings to bow, and can't see or feel which note we're singing. We must be able to hear song forms and chord progressions in order to improvise on them. And, like our instrumental counterparts, we need to internalize hundreds of melodic fragments in order to have a musical vocabulary.

The next steps will speed up that process. Be patient, memorize these exercises, and the music will become part of your mental data bank. With practice, you'll become comfortable singing variations on the exercises with the accompaniment track. It's amazing how many different melodies are waiting to be sung!

The following steps apply to learning to improvise over any chord progression, and are illustrated in the *Jazz Blues Workout* on page 62.

Chorus 1: Write out and sing the roots.

As we discovered in "Four Steps to Singing Blues Changes," the root of a chord is the lowest note of the chord and corresponds to the letter name of the chord. To learn a new chord progression, write down the root of each chord on a piece of staff paper, using whole notes when the chord lasts for one measure, and half notes when there are two chords per measure. Put them in the lowest comfortable part of your range, because you'll be adding chord tones above them later. Sing this several times at 60 beats per minute (use a metronome or just follow the ticks of the second hand on your watch) until you've memorized it. Vary the rhythms to make it swing.

Chorus 2: Write out and sing the roots and thirds.

After you've memorized the roots, the next step is to learn the thirds, which give the chord its basic color of either major or minor. There are two types of thirds: a major third, which is four half steps above the root, and a minor third, which is three half steps above the root. If a chord symbol includes a small "m," a "dim," an "o" or a "ø" after the letter name, the third is minor. In all other cases it is major.

Write out the roots again and fill in the thirds. If the root was a whole note, the root and third should now be half notes. If the root was a half note, the root and third should now be quarter notes. If the root was a quarter note, the root and third should now be eighth notes. Sing the line you've written at a slow tempo. Again, vary the rhythms to make it swing.

Chorus 3: Write out and sing the first three notes of each scale.

Fill in the passing tone between the roots and thirds and sing the first three notes of the scale. Memorize this and you'll hear the harmonic progression even more clearly.

Chorus 4: Write out and sing the chord tones to each chord, from root to seventh, then improvise with them.

Chorus 5: Improvise a solo using both scale and chord tones.

Jazz Blues Workout

roots

chorus 1

Doot doo day — doot doo day — doot doo day — doo doo
doot doo day — doo doo doot doo day — doo doo
doot doo day — doot doo day — doot doo day — doo doo

roots and thirds

chorus 2

doo doo — doo doo — doo doo — doot doot doot doot
doo doo — doo doo doo doo doo doo — doo doo doo doo
doo doo — doo doo — doo doo — doo doo doo da

first three notes

chorus 3

doo boo day — doo boo day — doo boo day — doo boo dayt doo boo dayt
doo boo day — doo buh dayt da buh dayt doo boo day — da ba dayt da ba dit
doo boo day — da boo day — doo boo day — da ba dat doo ba doo

Judy Niemack's *Hear It and Sing It! Exploring the Blues* — Chapter 5: Jazz Blues

solo with chord tones

chorus 4

G7

Vwee va vway va do da dow — va daht va vwee va

Dm7 G7 C7 C7 C#dim7

da voo vwee — do do dee dee deet dee sa — doo doo dlow bay

G7 Bm7♭5 E7 A7

dit doot da ba boo dlay dow va da va day do day —

D7 G7 Am7 D7

— day dot day bo da ba dot day ba doo ba doo bay oo ba —

solo with scale and chord tones

chorus 5

G7

doo va day day dee va deev doo ee a da doo ee a da ba do va da va

Dm7 G7 C7 C7 C#dim7

doo va doo vap swee — va doo ee a doot dlay dla va dee dla vay

G7/D Bm7♭5 E7 A7

doo va da vay oo ya do doo va dee da da sha va dee da doo va do ya

D7 G7 Am7 D7

doo va doo vay ee dow so vwee va oh vay dla do bee bee yow —

A common reaction to the excitement and occasional anxiety of improvising is to move directly from one idea to another in an attempt to be "interesting." This results in solos with many ideas but little direction. One way to create an interesting yet artistic solo is to repeat and develop your melodic motif before moving on to the next one.

A motif is defined as a short sequence of notes forming the basis for development in a piece of music. It can be repeated several times, starting on a different beats, sung in sequences (moving the motif up or down a tone within the scale), or using melodic variations. Remember, jazz is music of theme and variation: don't leave your motifs behind until you've explored them. Practice inventing short melodic motifs and developing them with the accompaniment track.

Developing Motifs on a Jazz Blues 27 28

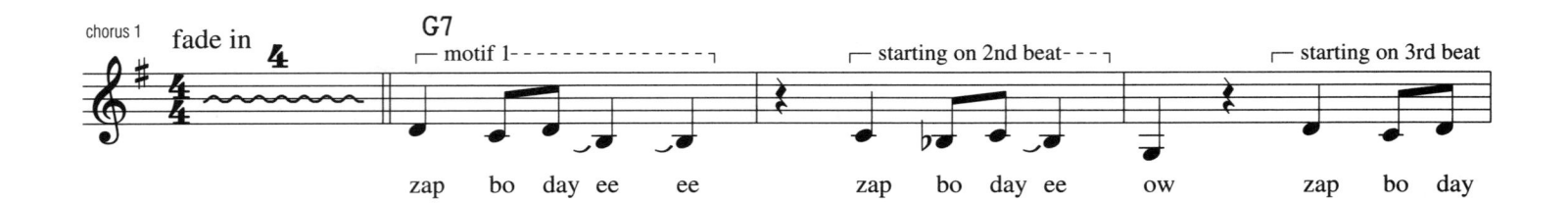

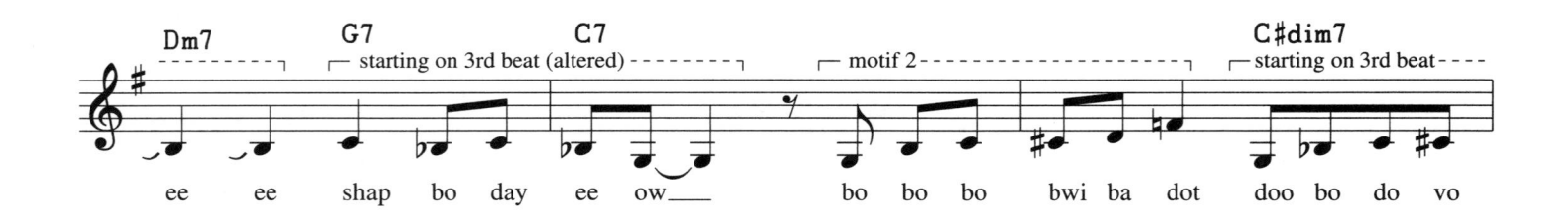

D7
conclusion
G7
Am7
D7
soot vlee dl lee dow
doo doo dwee n dee dee ee ow
chorus 2
G7
motif 3
repetition with different intervals
za vway
ba doo va ba doo ya
doot sa
Dm7
G7
C7
melodic variation
C7
C#dim7
boo doo doo ba dwee yoo
dap bah
zo ba oo ba ba boo
G7
repetition with wider intervals
Bm7b5
E7
A7
conclusion
sweep sah
sa ba doo dle oo bee
deet dat dlay dlow
D7(#11)
G7
Am7
D7
bweep bap bwayp doo dow

New Concept (for a Blue Planet) was originally an instrumental called *Blue Concept*, written by bebop saxophonist Gigi Gryce. Mastering the exercises on pages 62-65 will prepare you to improvise on this song, since they are based on the same chord progression.

In the vocal track, you'll hear me trading fours with one of the top jazz drummers on the New York scene, Victor Lewis. Listen to how we repeat, develop and react to each other's rhythmic ideas. Trading fours is more than just improvising four bars, it involves listening to and responding to the other soloist.

The expanded accompaniment-only track provides you with two choruses for the lyrics followed by three solo choruses for practicing improvisation. After the solo choruses there are four choruses of trading fours, and two more lyric choruses at the end.

Use the three choruses of improvisation to practice building the intensity of your solo. Start with a simple phrase, then vary and develop it, gradually letting the solo grow in rhythmic complexity, range and dynamics.

When you practice trading fours, try to hear and repeat a rhythmic motif from each drum solo, adding a melody to it. You'll develop the habit of listening to and responding to what your drummer is playing when you trade fours with a live band.

Judy Niemack's *Hear It and Sing It! Exploring the Blues*   Chapter 5: Jazz Blues   67

vocal lead sheet
& transcription
G

NEW CONCEPT (FOR A BLUE PLANET) 29 30
Instrumentally known as "Blue Concept"

Music by Gigi Gryce
Lyric by Judy Niemack

Medium swing (♩ = ca. 160)

Intro — G6 Gdim7 Am7 Gdim7 G6 Gdim7 Am7
f
D pedal

We've got to

4-feel
G7

try and find a brand new con - cept, a way of
years we thought that we were win - ners, and we de -

melody
G7   Dm7   G7   C7

walk - ing through the world with love and re - spect, 'cause if we fo - cus on a peace - ful
served to live the life that vic - tor - y brings, but there's a lim - it to the joy that

Piano C7   C#dim7   G7

out - look we can be - gin _____   to leave a
each new pur - chase can give _____   and when the

Bm7♭5 E7   A7   D7   G6

bet - ter place ___ be - hind us ___   on our love - ly blue plan -
fin - al act ___ is o - ver, ___   hey, you can't take it with

|1. |2. to fours (vocal track)
                                               to solo choruses (accompaniment-only track)

(G6) Em7 Am7 D7   (G6) Em7 Am7 D7

 ___ et.   For man - y ___ you.

Copyright © 1956 (renewed 1984), 2011 Second Floor Music and Twenty-Eighth Street Music

68 Chapter 5: Jazz Blues

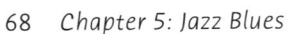

fours with Drums

chorus 1

Bi d bi d bi d bi d bi d bow d bway bway dow dow d doo day

sho da bay oo ba doo bay a yo dee dloo dlay dlay dlay loo dle lay da doo bay ay a doo day

chorus 2

sa ba doo va dayt day sa va doo va dayt day sha vo vay vay ool ya doot dweet dayt doo dow

chorus 3

sip di dip di di di dip di d dip vee doo vo vwee a doo voo vwee va doo n day dee ow

ba doo lo dop do blee ba yoo ba doo ba dayt veet dov - vee dop bwee

Judy Niemack's *Hear It and Sing It! Exploring the Blues* — Chapter 5: Jazz Blues

chorus 4 Drums

ba — bay a ba doo ba ya bay ya ba doo dle lee blee slee ba oo va oo ba day d bway dee

Drums

ow I must ad-

out melody

mit my nose is to the grind-stone, and so I
talk a-bout a brand new con-cept. A time to

sing this song for me as much as for you. I on-ly know we can't de-ny that
cel-e-brate the beau-ty right here on earth 'cause it's a mir-a-cle that we've got

Piano

some-thing's rad-i-c'lly wrong. We're hav-ing
such a won-der-ful place, and if we

hail-storms here in sum-mer: flow-ers bloom-ing in win-
learn to treat it gent-ly, we can live here a long,

1. ter. It's time to
2. long time.

CHAPTER 6: BIRD BLUES

During the Bebop era of the mid-1940s, alto saxophonist Charlie Parker, nicknamed "Bird," and trumpeter Dizzy Gillespie invented a blues progression using a descending root movement, with a cycle of chords moving in fourths upward. Variations of this progression became known as the "Bird Blues," which is also referred to as the II - V Blues. Parker composed a melody called *Blues for Alice* using a similar progression.

The II and V chords in these progressions are often altered to fit the melody, so they may not always look exactly like the progression below.

BIRD BLUES CHORD PROGRESSION

Cmaj7	Bm7♭5 E7	Am7 D7	Gm7 C7
Fmaj7	Fm7 B♭7	Em7 A7	E♭m7 A♭7
Dm7	G7	Em7 A7	Dm7 G7

Charlie Parker

Guide tones

Bird Blues chord progressions are more complex than traditional blues progressions and more difficult to improvise over. One of the best ways for singers to learn complex chord progressions like these is by singing "guide tone" lines. Guide tones can be loosely defined as notes that guide the ear from chord to chord. Often they are the third and seventh of the chords, which lead the ear to resolve to a note a semitone higher or lower. The seventh of the dominant chord is also called the "leading tone" and tends to resolve to the third of the tonic. Learning to sing the following guide tone lines will ground you in this important leading tone movement in the Bird Blues.

To create a guide tone line, start with the third of the first chord and move to the third or seventh of the next chord, whichever is closer. Then fill in the line with passing tones.

Repeat the process, starting on the seventh of the first chord, moving to the closest third or seventh.

Practice improvising melodies, staying very close to guide tone lines.

I wrote the following song, *In Flight,* to illustrate the use of typical bebop phrases on a Bird Blues. I enjoyed singing it so much that I wrote a lyric to it and added it to my repertoire! It is based on a **II - V** progression with some variations. I used the ♭5 chord in the second measure because the melody has a ♭5 in it. In the fourth measure, I've used the scale tones of the altered scale, so you'll see the symbol **alt**.

On *In Flight,* I've sung two choruses of lyrics, then four choruses of guide tone exercises, which you'll find starting on page 74. Then I traded fours with pianist Norman Simmons, and ended with two more choruses of the lyrics. When you practice with the accompaniment-only track, see if you can pick up on Norman's melodic ideas and use them in your improvised fours.

I've changed the melody on the "out chorus" (the last chorus on page 73), in order to give you an idea of how you can vary the melody while keeping the lyrics intact.

72 Chapter 6: Bird Blues   Judy Niemack's *Hear It and Sing It! Exploring the Blues*

vocal lead sheet
E♭

In Flight ①❸ (CD#2)

Judy Niemack

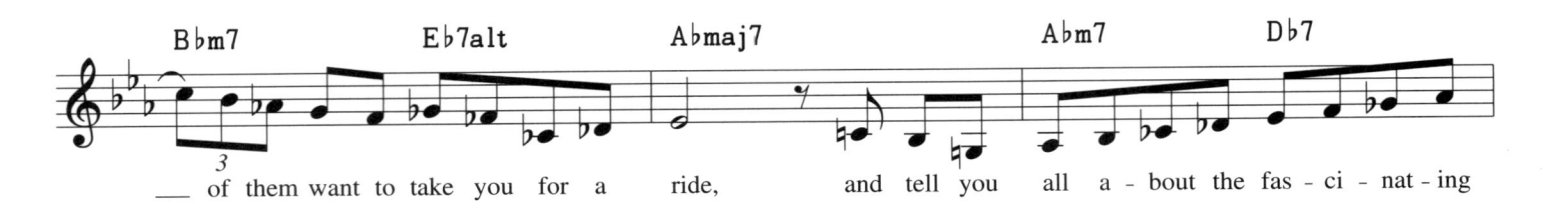

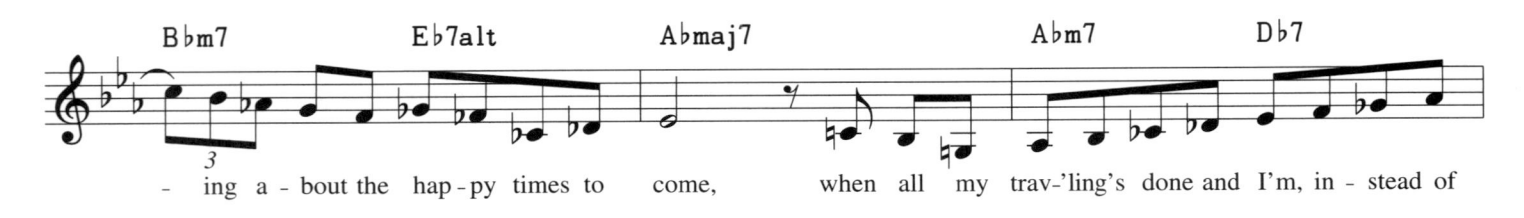

Intro (instrumental)

| Am7♭5 | D7(♯9) | Gm7 | C7(♭9) | Fm7 Gm7 A♭maj7 Adim7 | B♭9(13) | E7 |

f

melody chorus 1

| E♭maj7 | Dm7♭5 | G7 | Cm7 | F7 |

Fly-ing a-round the world__ you meet an aw-ful lot of peo-ple.__ Some

| B♭m7 | E♭7alt | A♭maj7 | A♭m7 | D♭7 |

__ of them want to take you for a ride, and tell you all a-bout the fas-ci-nat-ing

| Gm7 | C7 | F♯m7 B7 | Fm7 |

things that they've done,__ is-n't it fun? Ac-tu'l-ly all I want to

| B♭7 | Gm7 | C7 | Fm7 | B♭7 | *last time*

do is get the next con-nec-tion straight back to you,__ but I've got to keep on trav'-ling 'til I'm

melody chorus 2

| E♭maj7 | Dm7♭5 | G7 | Cm7 | F7 |

through. That's why when I'm in flight I al-ways try to take it eas-y,___ think-

| B♭m7 | E♭7alt | A♭maj7 | A♭m7 | D♭7 |

-ing a-bout the hap-py times to come, when all my trav'-ling's done and I'm, in-stead of

Copyright © 2011 Second Floor Music

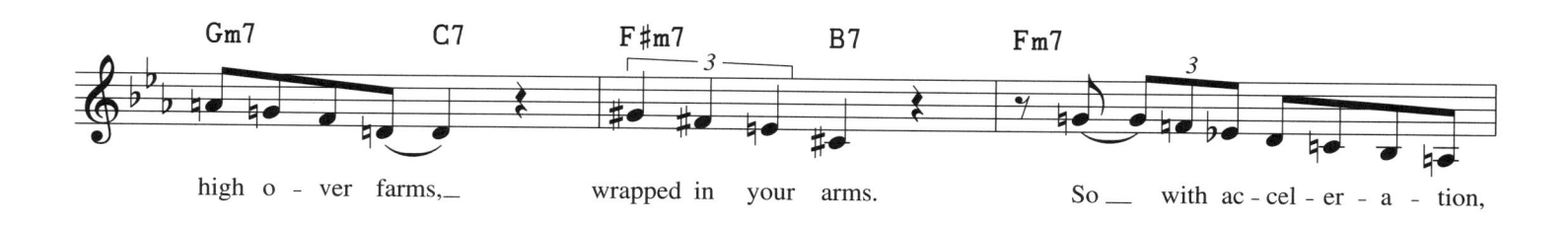

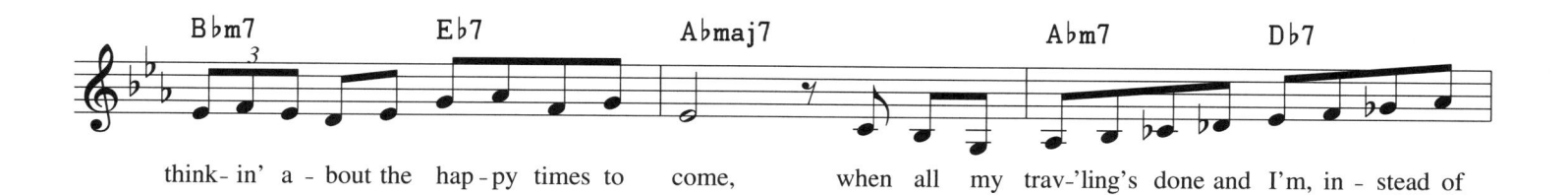

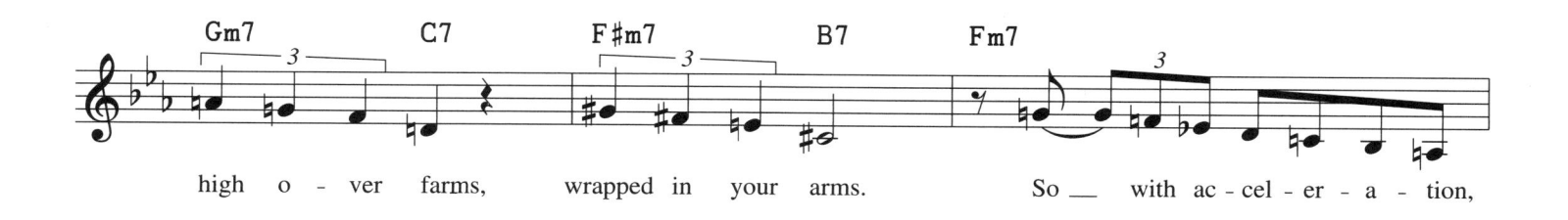

high o-ver farms,__ wrapped in your arms. So__ with ac-cel-er-a-tion,

high-er el-e-va-tion and the prom-ise of love,__ I keep drift-ing through di-aph-a-nous clouds a-

out melody chorus 2 last time

through. That's why when I'm in flight__ I al-ways try to take it eas-y,

think-in' a-bout the hap-py times to come, when all my trav-'ling's done and I'm, in-stead of

high o-ver farms, wrapped in your arms. So__ with ac-cel-er-a-tion,

high-er el-e-va-tion and the prom-ise of love,__ I keep drift-ing through di-aph-a-nous clouds a-

bove. And it's great, we've not late, I can't wait _____ to get home.

starting on thirds and moving to sevenths

rhythmic variations

starting on sevenths and moving to thirds

Judy Niemack's *Hear It and Sing It! Exploring the Blues* — Chapter 6: Bird Blues — 75

improvising with sevenths moving to thirds

chorus 4

doo day doo day doo   da day doo dow __   da day doo dow __   da day doo dow

doot doo   dwee doo ___   doo doo   sha dwee doo __   shoo dwee dah __

shap da bay doo wah ___   shop bay doo dle ee ba bwee ah ___

trading fours

chorus 5

Piano solos

Shoo-wee-a da-ee-a da-ee-a da-ee-a doo-ee-a doo-ee-a doo-ee-a

doo-ee-a doo-ee-a doo-ee-a doo-ee-a dehp dop w-wee ah ___

Piano solos

shav va

chorus 6

da vay doodle ay _   va dool ya do va doo va yoo va doo vay dool ya doo vo yoo va dee va dool ya da

Piano solos

D.S. 𝄋 *al* ⊕

say doot bay dahp __ bwee ow __   sha do ba bwee ba da-ee-a ba dwee da doo ba yah

TRADING FOURS WITH SHEILA JORDAN ② ❸

Sheila Jordan's first great influence was Charlie Parker. Indeed, most of her influences have been instrumentalists rather than singers. I asked Sheila to sing on these Bird Blues changes with me. You'll hear us trading fours; it was fun to play off her ideas! Try trading fours with a horn player or another singer with the accompaniment track.

1: Judy sings a pattern based on a descending minor third.

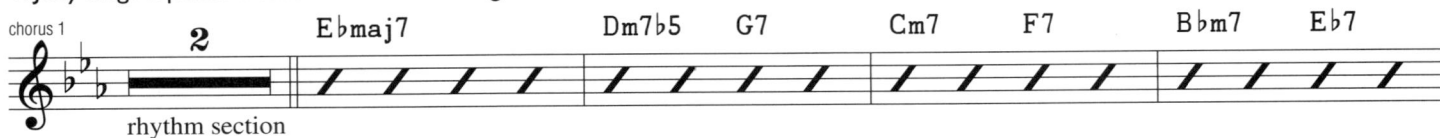

chorus 1 | Ebmaj7 | Dm7b5 G7 | Cm7 F7 | Bbm7 Eb7
rhythm section

2: Sheila sings an ascending minor third idea, then a descending phrase with triplets ("doo-dlee-ya, doo-dlee-ya").

Abmaj7 | Abm7 Db7 | Gm7 C7 | F#m7 B7

3: Judy repeats Sheila's last two notes, develops it into a phrase, then sings an arpeggiated chord up to her higher range.

Fm7 | Bb7(b13) | Gm C7 | Fm7 Bb7

1: Sheila starts a half step higher than the highest note in Judy's previous phrase, then brings it back down to speech range with a typical Charlie Parker motif ending with a blues scale phrase.

chorus 2 | Ebmaj7 | Dm7b5 G7 | Cm7 F7 | Bbm7 Eb7

2: Judy repeats Sheila's blues scale phrase, developing and changing it.

Abmaj7 | Abm7 Db7 | Gm7 C7 | F#m7 B7

3: Sheila takes Judy's last idea and develops it, finishing off with a motif based on approaching a note from a half step below ("chromatic approach").

Fm7 | Bb7(b13) | Gm C7 | Fm7 Bb7

Judy Niemack's *Hear It and Sing It! Exploring the Blues* Chapter 6: Bird Blues   77

1. Judy takes the chromatic approach fragment and sequences it eight times, from her high to low range.

chorus 3 | Ebmaj7 | Dm7b5 G7 | Cm7 F7 | Bbm7 Eb7 |

2. Sheila descends to the depths of her range, and then comes back up with some original sounds!

| Abmaj7 | Abm7 Db7 | Gm7 C7 | F#m7 B7 |

3. Judy starts with a turn and sings a double-time phrase down the scale, then comes back up with chromatic approach notes.

| Fm7 | Bb7(b13) | Gm C7 | Fm7 Bb7 |

1. Sheila surprises Judy with a compliment...

chorus 4 | Ebmaj7 | Dm7b5 G7 | Cm7 F7 | Bbm7 Eb7 |

2. Judy replies...

| Abmaj7 | Abm7 Db7 | Gm7 C7 | F#m7 B7 |

3. Sheila rhymes it!

| Fm7 | Bb7(b13) | Gm C7 | Fm7 Bb7 |

fade out

Chapter 7: Blues Scale on Standards

"I can't sing a blues—just a right-out blues—but I can put the blues in whatever I sing. I might sing Send In The Clowns, *and I might stick a little bluesy part in it, or any song...."*
                              Sarah Vaughan

You can always use the blues scale with a blues, but you can also use it with other songs. Although it can be used over any chord, it's usually over a dominant seventh or minor seventh chord. Jazz singers, like Sarah Vaughan, sometimes use the blues scale in their interpretations of standards and songs that aren't blues by definition. Like a distinctive spice, blue notes are most effective when used sparingly.

Here's an example of an improvised solo, sung over chord changes similar to those of George Gershwin's *Summertime*. Notice how well the C blues scale and the C minor pentatonic scale work on this song.

Use the accompaniment track to experiment with blues scale use on a well-known standard chord progression.

The following jazz standards work well with a touch of the blues scale. Start the blues scale on the root or "tonic" of the key the song is in.

Angel Eyes (Matt Dennis, Earl Brent)
Black Coffee (Paul Francis Webster, Sonny Burke)
Cry Me A River (Arthur Hamilton)
Gee Baby, Ain't I Good to You (Don Redman, Andy Razaf)
Georgia on My Mind (Hoagy Carmichael, Stuart Gorrell)
God Bless the Child (Billie Holiday, Arthur Herzog, Jr.)
Dat Dere (Bobby Timmons, Oscar Brown, Jr.)
Fever (John Davenport, Eddie Cooley)
Moanin' (Bobby Timmons, Jon Hendricks)
Song For My Father (Horace Silver)
Stormy Weather (Harold Arlen, Ted Koehler)
Willow Weep For Me (Ann Ronell)

transcription
B♭

Summer Blues ④❺

Medium swing

Judy Niemack

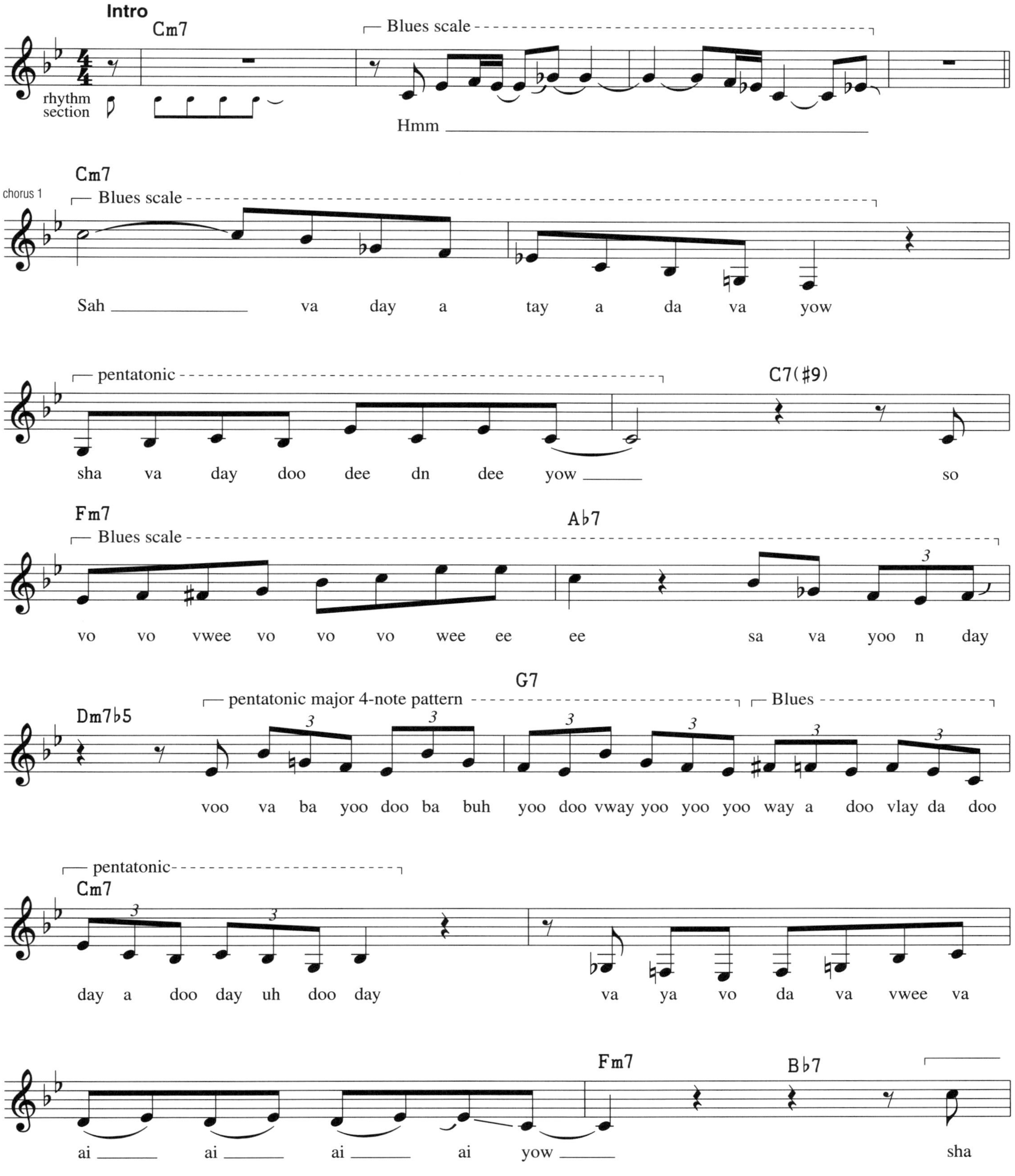

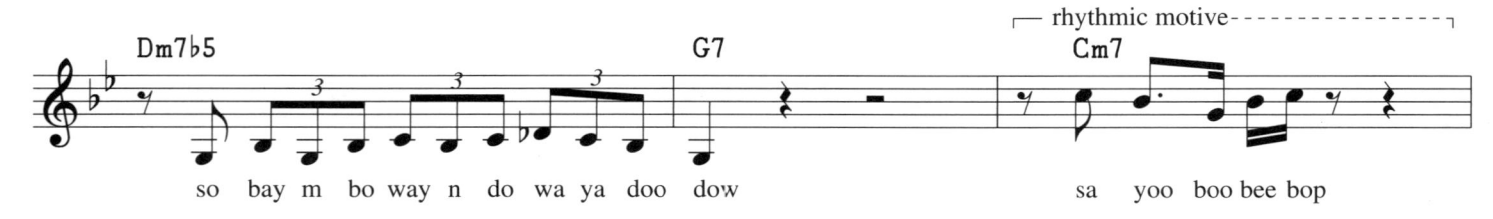

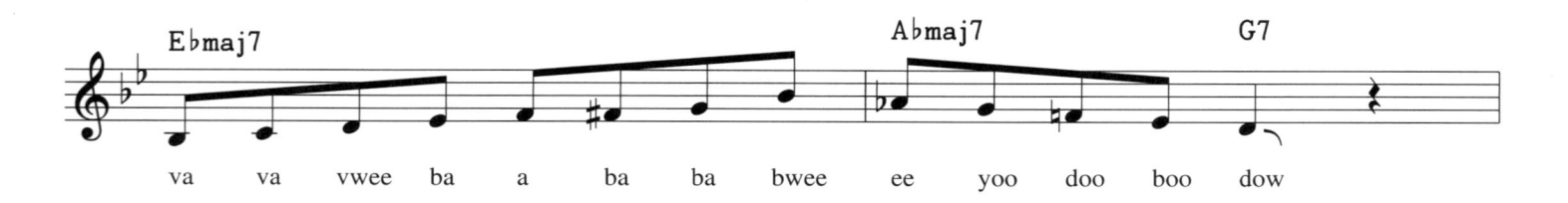

Chapter 7: Blues Scale on Standards

Sheet music — Eb major scale / chromatic scale passage with scat syllables

Ebmaj7 — Eb major scale
da voo vwee oo voo vwee a voo vwee a voo vwee ah
Abmaj7 G7#5 — chromatic scale
sha va va

Cm7
vwee o da vo vay o da vo vwee yoo dow

chorus 2
Cm7
sa —— doop bway ee boo bay boo bi dit bo bop bay ee ya dat dow

C7(#9)   **Fm7**   **Ab7**
—— sa bwee — ba bwee ya doo bo bwee ya da yow ——

Dm7b5   **G7**   — rhythmic motive —   **Cm7**
so bay m bo way n do wa ya doo dow   sa yoo boo bee bop

Fm7   **Bb7**
sa ya n deedop   sa ya boo di dip   blay —— ya doo dow   so

Ebmaj7   **Abmaj7**   **G7**
va va vwee ba a ba ba bwee   ee yoo doo boo dow

Judy Niemack's *Hear It and Sing It! Exploring the Blues* Chapter 7: Blues Scale on Standards 81

CHAPTER 8: BLUES WITH A BRIDGE

One day, a close friend of mine told me that we'd have to put our friendship "on ice" for a while. My feelings were hurt, but the phrase kept coming back to me, and I decided to write a blues. I wrote the melody and Jeanfrançois Prins re-harmonized a 12-measure blues, we added a bridge, and the *Ice White Blues* was born.

Ice White Blues

vocal lead sheet B

Music by Judy Niemack and Jeanfrançois Prins
Lyric by Judy Niemack

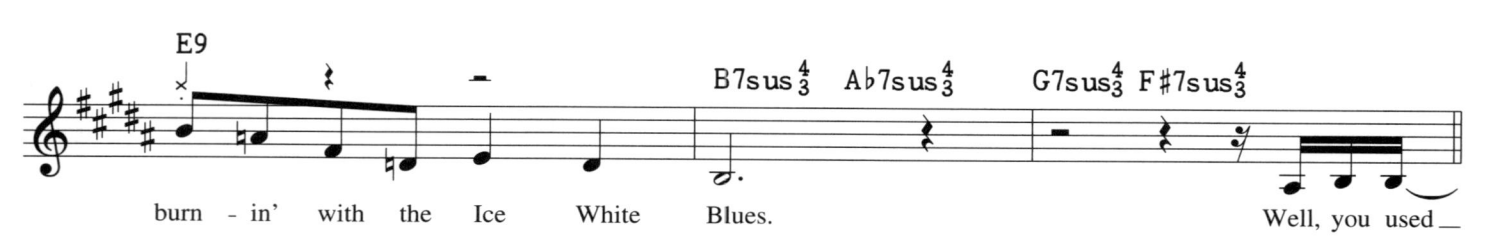

Latin funk (♩ = ca. 94)
Intro (double-time feel)

Lyrics:

I remember how you told me: "You gotta keep your love on ice."

You think that I'll be waiting here so you can burn me twice?

Well, you left me something, it's something that I've got to lose,

you left my cold heart burnin',

burnin' with the Ice White Blues. Well, you used —

Copyright © 2004, 2011 Second Floor Music

Judy Niemack's Hear It and Sing It! Exploring the Blues — Chapter 8: Blues with a Bridge — 83

chorus 2: _____ to tell___ me, ev-'ry day, I was the world ___ to you, ___
and if I ___ ev-er went a-way, what would your poor heart _ do?
Well, you turned the ta-bles, and I'm a-bout to blow _____ a fuse. _____
You left my cold heart burn-in',
burn-in' with the Ice White Blues._____

bridge: And now you call and say you're com-in' back _ to me, ___
tell-in' me __ that things could be just like they used to be. But
you've been gone so long and hon-ey, you __ must pay __ the price, ___ 'cause
now my heart is fro-zen, it's as white as ice. ____ Now

84 Chapter 8: Blues with a Bridge

chorus 3

love be-gins with ro-ses, scar-let, crim-son, ru-by hues, and love'll take you pla-ces with a prom-ise to a-muse, but when you end up lone-ly, feel-in' like you're born to lose, you'll find your cold heart burn-in', burn-in' with the Ice White Blues.

bridge

And now you call and say you're com-in' back to me, You're tell-in' me that things will be just like they used to be. But on the day you left me, well my heart, it turned to ice, and since I'm feel-in' noth-in' here's some free ad-vice. Well, if the

chorus 4
B7sus4/3 D7sus4/3 C#7sus4/3 C7sus4/3
one who says he loves_ you starts to leave a cou - ple clues,_ like he's
B7sus4/3 F7(13)
on the phone at mid - night, says he's giv - in' in - ter - views,_ well, you can
E9
bet your bot - tom dol - lar you're head - ed for some se - ri - ous dues._
B7sus4/3
You'll find your
F#7#5(#9)
cold ___ heart ___ burn - in', ___ you'll find your
F#7#5(#9)
cold heart _ burn - in', ___ you'll find your
F#7#5(#9)
cold ___ heart ___ burn - in', ___
slower
Ab7 A7 Bb7 B7
burn - in' with the Ice White Blues.

CHAPTER 9: ORIGINAL BLUES LYRICS

Ice White Blues was inspired by the unexpected use of a common phrase. But blues can also document political or historical events, like Bessie Smith's *Boll Weevil Blues*, about an infestation of boll weevils that ruined the cotton crops, or *Backwater Blues* about the great Mississippi floods. There are hundreds of traditional blues lyrics to choose from in the books listed in the Resources chapter. Look for songs that have lyrics that appeal to you, or use them as inspiration to write your own lyrics.

Sheila Jordan's music has earned praise from many critics, particularly for her ability to improvise entire lyrics. Scott Yanow describes her as "one of the most consistently creative of all jazz singers." She tells her students, "Don't be afraid to take chances. This music will live forever, but you have to give it away to keep it." She improvised these blues lyrics for aspiring jazz and blues singers.

Sing your own story with the accompaniment track.

SHEILA'S BLUES ⑧ ⑨
by Sheila Jordan

1. It started with the blues, yeah.
I know you all are gonna pay some dues.
Hey, singers! Hey, swingers! It started with the blues.
Yeah, yeah, yeah, yeah, yeah, yeah, yeah.
You gotta sing your song.
Lemme tell ya, I'm here to help ya, as you go along.

2. Well, you can talk about what you did last night,
whether you had a good time, or whether you got in a fight.
Talk about the day. Hey, hey, waddaya say?
Tell me how you feel, yeah, but you gotta make sure that you're really real.
Make it up as you go along, that's how you sing a blues song.
I'm gonna show you what I mean:

3. Well, I was born in Detroit, Michigan, back in 1928.
Yeah, I was born in Detroit, Michigan,
November the eighteenth, 1928, Mickey Mouse's birthday.
But my mother she was only sixteen years old and she couldn't raise me.
So she sent me to live with my grandparents in a small coal mining town in Pennsylvania State.

Copyright © 1984, 2011 Second Floor Music

4. You see what I mean? All you gotta do is sing.
Sing about where you came from, and maybe about your birthday.
But it really doesn't always have to be that way.
Just tell me what you feel, as long as you make it real. Hey, singers, singers,
singers, singers, singers, singers sing your song,
and the band will play, and groove as you sing along.

5. Well, getting back to me,
I used to sing with the miners in the beer garden up the street every
Saturday night.
The miners used to sit around and drink their beer and whiskey
and sing their songs, "You are my sunshine, my only sunshine."
Rarely, rarely, rarely, rarely, rarely, rarely, rarely, rarely, rarely, rarely, rarely,
rarely, rarely, rarely, rarely, rarely, rarely, rarely, rarely, rarely,

6. Rarely, rarely, rarely did they ever fight.
Do you know what I mean, singers?
You gotta do your thing, do your thing and make it swing.
Yeah, yeah, yeah, it's all up to you, I think you'll know what to do.
Just tell everybody how you feel, 'cause, hey, that's the real deal.

7. Getting back to me, well, I moved back to Detroit, Michigan, when I
was about fourteen.
Hangin' down at the "Club Sudan," well, that was everybody's scene.
You didn't have to be twenty-one years old to get in there.
It was just a place for kids to play and sing.

8. Well, we were always chasin' Charlie Parker.
I think he wrote that song for us— "Chasin' the Bird," "Chasin' the Bird,"
"Chasin' the Bird."
When he used to play at the "Club El Cino," where you had to be
twenty-one years old to get in,
I used to forge my mother's birth certificate.
All I had was a veil, high-heeled shoes that were killing my feet.
I was gonna get in the door to hear the Bird, but the man said,
"Hey, kid! Hey kid! Hey kid! Hey, little white girl,

9. Go home and do your homework!"
So we went round in the alley and we were sitting on the garbage cans.
Bird! Bird! Bird! Bird! Bird knew we were there, and he opened up the
door, and he played his heart out for me.

Oh, what a treat, what a treat, what a treat, what a treat, what a treat, what a treat, what a treat, what a treat, what a treat for a fourteen-year-old kid that loved jazz.

10. Now I'm gonna let Jeanfrançois play, and he'll make, make, make your day.
Tell us about it!

11. (Jeanfrançois Prins guitar solo)

12. Oh yeah, singers, I forgot to tell you,
when the instrumentalists play, don't forget to listen!
Don't let your mind wander off.
You know what I mean, you gotta be on the list'nin' scene.
I know you can do what I say. Hey!

13. Well, if it wasn't for jazz music, I wouldn't be alive today. Oh, no!
If it wasn't for jazz music, I wouldn't be alive today.
Because back when I was just a skinny little teenager by the nickname of Jeannie Dawson, runnin' down on John R. in Detroit, Michigan, to buy all those fantastic bebop records, so I could hear Thelonious Monk and Miles Davis and Max Roach and Ray Brown and Dizzy Gillespie and Miles Davis and Fats Navarro and Kenny Dorham and Billie Holiday and Sarah Vaughan and Ella Fitzgerald and Count Basie and Duke Ellington, and of course, Lester Young, the "Prez" (You can do it kids, I'm tellin' you!)—
I wouldn't be up here singing, and tellin' you that you should do the blues today!

Chapter 10: Vocalese Blues

Vocalese is the art of setting lyrics to recorded jazz instrumental solos, creating an entirely new form of the work, one that tells an interesting story while retaining the integrity of the music. The word "vocalese" was coined by jazz critic Leonard Feather to describe the first Lambert, Hendricks & Ross album, "Sing a Song of Basie." On that recording, Lambert, Hendricks & Ross used overdubbing so that the three singers could replace the entire horn section of the Count Basie Orchestra. Jon Hendricks wrote lyrics to the horn parts and solos and a new art form was born. "Vocalese," a pun on the classical term "vocalise," combines the idea of jazz vocals with that of a new language (indicated by the suffix -"ese").

Vocalese is not scat, although one is commonly mistaken for the other. Vocalese is adding words to what were previously instrumental pieces (i.e., big band arrangements or improvised solos); scat singing is a technique where nonsense syllables are sung to improvised melodies.

Vocalese lyrics are often either elaborate storytelling or a tribute to the musician who originally recorded the solo. For example, Annie Ross's *Twisted,* based on a solo by Wardell Gray, tells a fantastic story about a young lady's relationship with her psychiatrist: "My analyst told me I was right out of my head. The way he described it, he said I'd be better dead than live. . . ." Eddie Jefferson's lyrics to Coleman Hawkins' famous recording of *Body and Soul* are a tribute to Hawkins, and sing his praises: "Don't you know, he was the king of saxophone, yes indeed, he was. . . ." Joni Mitchell's lyrics to *Goodbye Pork Pie Hat:* "When Charlie speaks of Lester, you know someone great has gone . . ." are a loosely interpreted version of Booker Ervin's solo on the original Charles Mingus recording. The lyric combines a tribute to Lester Young and Mingus with musings about racism, progress and music.

After learning several blues vocalese lyrics, like Annie Ross's *Twisted,* King Pleasure's *Parker's Mood* and Joni Mitchell's *Goodbye Pork Pie Hat,* I decided to try my hand at vocalese writing. I love Dexter Gordon's wonderful solo on *Home Run,* so I wrote a lyric to the melody and the entire saxophone solo. It's all about a guy who ought to *Run Home* and appreciate what he's got!

Here's a tip for getting the words to flow at this brisk tempo: focus on the consonants at the beginning of the words, and really spit them out. Consonants help to propel the musical line, and in an up-tempo vocalese, it's a challenge to be understood. Don't be afraid to exaggerate your pronunciation a bit.

90 | Chapter 10: Vocalese Blues

Run Home
Instrumentally known as "Home Run"

solo vocalese
Dexter Gordon's melody
& tenor sax solo
C

Music by Dexter Gordon
Lyric by Judy Niemack

Medium up swing (♩ = ca. 170)

Intro

Run, boy, run. Have some fun.

When you're done, run home! Now you're head-in' for the

melody
chorus 1 & 2

bar and you're dres-sin' like a star.
fine, of-fers you a glass of wine,

While you're cruis-in' in your car, Ba-by won-ders where you
wants to have a lit-tle fun, wants to spend a lit-tle

are. If you want to sleep to-night, you'd bet-ter run home.
time. If your ba-by treats you right, you'd bet-ter run home.

|1.
Some-one's look-in' might-y

|2.
So you had a lous-y day,

Copyright © 1961 (renewed 1989), 2005, 2011 Second Floor Music

nothin' seemed to go your way. Just re-mem-ber what I say: If you play, you got-ta pay! If you think you wan-na stay, well, then you'd bet-ter run home.

Solo (4-feel)

Go on home and tell her what you're wor-ried 'bout, 'cause when you do you're gon-na find real quick she real-ly does be-lieve that you're the top. And, in case you hadn't no-ticed, love is like a bon-us. Give some at-ten-tion, get some af-fec-tion. Did-n't you ev-er won-der why no-thin' makes you hap-py? Take a good look, o-pen up your eyes and see!

I re-mem-ber how it used to feel so good when you used to take her out on the town, and you'd run in-to a friend, or some-one you just met, who gave her the eye, she'd pass him by. Now she's home, waiting all alone, hoping you'll appear just like a knight in shining armor. If

chorus 3
you could ask her what she's feelin', you would find it so revealin', and the message would be healin'. You could hold your head up high, knowing that she loves you, you dummy. Silly as though it seems, when she calls you on the phone maybe you should tell her that she's really and truly a gem, or even tell her she's a treasure.

chorus 4
Think what you're gonna do, think it thru. Take a step way back and while you're waitin', check it out. No one but you knows the answer, though I've been preachin', I just got to say what I think is true. Listen to me when I say,

chorus 5
shout chorus
Bass
C7(13)/E
she's been wait - ing all the day.
When the cat has gone a - way,
F7(13)/A
then the mice be - gin to play.
A7/E
If you want a mouse to stay,
well then, you'd best run home.
D7(♭9) G7
Now you're head - in' for the
out melody
C7(13)
bar
go,
Bass *simile* melody
and you're dres - sin' like a
like the wind you wan - na
star.
blow,
G7(♭9) C7
While you're cruis - in' in your car,
where you stop you'll nev - er know,
F7(13)
Ba - by won - ders where you
'cause you're go - in' with the
are.
flow.
If you want to sleep to -
When you come back down to -
night, you'd bet - ter run home.
earth, you'd bet - ter run home.
1.
2.
So you say you got - ta
Coda (Piano and Bass *simile* Intro)
Run, boy, run.
Have your fun.
When you're done,
run home!

Chapter 11: Odd-Meter Blues

One of the many possibilities in composing blues is to change the time signature from 4/4 to another time signature, for example 3/4, 5/4 or 7/4. These are called "odd-meter" time signatures. Several jazz blues composers, like jazz trombonist Julian Priester (with Tommy Turrentine and Oscar Brown, Jr.), have paved the way with songs like *Long As You're Living,* a blues in 5/4 (published in the "Sing Jazz!" book listed in the index). Another Julian Priester odd-meter blues, in 7/4, is instrumentally known as *Blues For Eros.* With my lyric about the legend of Aphrodite, Greek goddess of love and beauty, it's titled *Eros.*

When I was learning *Eros,* it was helpful for me to count it in four beats + three beats, although Julian Priester wrote the bass line in a pattern of two beats + three beats + two beats. Experiment with both ways of counting and see which one feels best for you.

It's a challenge to sing without a chordal instrument accompanying you. With the accompaniment track, you'll have an opportunity to hone this important skill.

The Meeting (page 100), instrumentally titled *Camp Meeting,* is a 3/4 blues by Johnny Griffin, evoking the excitement of an old-time revival meeting. After you've sung the melody, try using the lyrics as a springboard into your scat solo, reshaping the melody while singing the lyrics. You'll hear my example.

Judy Niemack's *Hear It and Sing It! Exploring the Blues* — Chapter 11: Odd-Meter Blues — 95

vocal lead sheet
C

EROS ⑫ ⑬
Instrumentally known as "Blues For Eros"

Music by Julian Priester
Lyric by Judy Niemack

Medium African feel

Intro (Bass only) — Horns:

Love's ___ the ___ pow'r ___ that ___ frees ___ the ___ mor - tal ___ soul.

(horns)

melody chorus 1
Bass *simile*

C7
Er - os ___ shoots with a per - fect aim. ___

F7
Pas - sion ___ scorch - es you with its ___ flame, ___

C7

Copyright © 1978, 2007, 2011 Second Floor Music

G7 F7
o - ver - pow - 'ring your e - mo - tion while de - mand - ing your de - vo - tion,
C7 (horns) D♭7
mf
lis - ten.
melody chorus 2
C7
Life's force fol - lows an un - seen plan.
F7 C7
Long - ing burns in the heart of man
G7 F7
lead - ing us to dance the dance, re - peat - ing pat - terns in a trance, con -
C7 D♭7
nect - ing.
chorus 3
C7
Pas - sion-ate god from a - bove, u - nit - ing our spir - its in love, you
F7 C7
fly on the wings of de - sire, ig - nit - ing our hearts with your fire. We're
G7 F7
search - ing for pleas - ure, some joy be - yond meas - ure, a

way to for-get that we're not here for-ev-er. We'll

chorus 4
fol-low you an-y-where, _____ Er - os.

Love is blind, we don't care, _____ Er - os.

Ma-ma said, "Don't you dare, _____ Er - os.

She's a hu-man, be-ware!" _____

When you saw Psy-che, she was so love-ly,

you could not leave her there. _____

chorus 5
Now, let me ex-plain how Aph-ro-di-te's son ___ took that girl a-way

and with the wed-ding done, ___ he loved her that night, but he con-cealed _ his name _

98   Chapter 11: Odd-Meter Blues   Judy Niemack's *Hear It and Sing It! Exploring the Blues*

out melody chorus 1
F7
C7
sweet - ness
whet - ting our ap - pe - tite.
G7
F7
Love can lead to des - per - a - tion or com - plete re - gen - er - a - tion,
C7
D♭7
heal - ing.
out melody chorus 2
C7
Wis - dom,
vir - tue and sac - ri - fice,
F7
C7
some say
they lead to par - a - dise.
G7
F7
If you love in mod - er - a - tion, you'll miss all the in - spi - ra - tion.
E9(♯11)
Er - os
E♭9(♯11)
D9(♯11)
calls you,
will you
D♭9(♯11)
C
Cmaj9(13 ♯11)
an - swer
now?

100   Chapter 11: Odd-Meter Blues   Judy Niemack's *Hear It and Sing It! Exploring the Blues*

THE MEETING ⑭ ⑮

vocal lead sheet
G

Instrumentally known as "Camp Meeting"

Medium up swing
Intro

Music by Johnny Griffin
Lyric by Judy Niemack

No time, got-ta run, me
late,
road.

and I've got no time for fun.
You know his love set me free

I'm gonna be on life's lone-ly

I can't miss this date.
from my heav-y load.

I've got to be there to join in the prayer, I won't make him
We're meet-ing to-day, it's so far a-way, but I'm com-ing

1. wait.   He came through for

2. home.

Copyright © 1962 (renewed 1990), 2007, 2011 Second Floor Music

Judy Niemack's *Hear It and Sing It! Exploring the Blues* — Chapter 11: Odd-Meter Blues

chorus 1

No time, _____ got-ta run, _____ you know I'm gon-na be late. I can't miss this date. I've got to be there ____ to join _____ in the prayer. _____ He came through __

chorus 2

__ for me on life's ____ lone-ly road. _____ His love _____ set me free from my heav-y load. We're meet-ing to-day, it's _____ so far a-way, _____ but I'm go-ing home. _____

102 Chapter 11: Odd-Meter Blues   Judy Niemack's *Hear It and Sing It! Exploring the Blues*

Judy Niemack's *Hear It and Sing It! Exploring the Blues*   Chapter 11: Odd-Meter Blues   103

got no time for fun. I can't miss this date. I've got to be there to join in the prayer, I won't make him wait. He came through for

out melody chorus 2

me on life's lone-ly road. You know his love set me free from my heav-y load. We're meet-ing to-day, it's so far a-way, but I'm com-in' home. I've got to be there to join in the prayer, no time to roam. The meet-ing's to-day, it's so far a-way, but I'm com-ing home, yeah, yeah.

Chapter 12: Chromatic Melody Blues

Blues That Soothe My Soul features a lovely chromatic melody composed by pianist Norman Simmons. It's instrumentally known as *Blues to Soothe*. Norman's music inspired me to write a lyric that might have been sung to one of Duke Ellington's ballads, back in the 1940s. Practice "laying back" on the beat when you sing this song. Relax and listen to the tempo the rhythm section lays down, then fall back on the beat a little, singing each word just a millisecond late.

On the accompaniment-only track there are three vocal choruses only (no piano solo), so instead of taking the second ending (to solos) on the first page, take the second ending (last time) on page 105.

Blues That Soothe My Soul

vocal lead sheet
Bb

Instrumentally known as "Blues To Soothe"

Music by Norman Simmons
Lyric by Judy Niemack

Slow swing (♩ = ca. 48)

Lyrics line 1:
pedal — I dream that you've gone as the night lin-gers on, — I try not to cry a - lone, — but I miss you. — So I sing, — and some-how the blues, they soothe — my soul.

Lyrics line 2:
— wait for your call, or your voice down the hall, — I sigh as I lie in bed, — 'cause I need you. — Then I dream, — and some-how the blues, they soothe — my soul.

Copyright © 1993, 2007, 2011 Second Floor Music

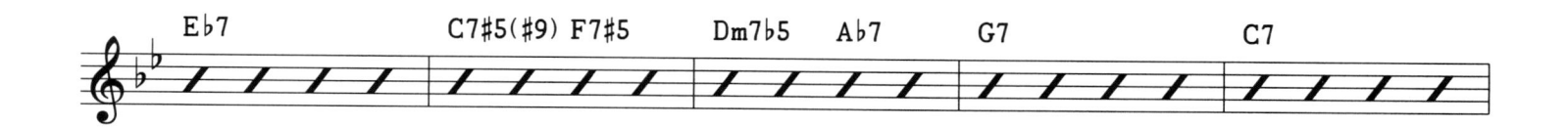

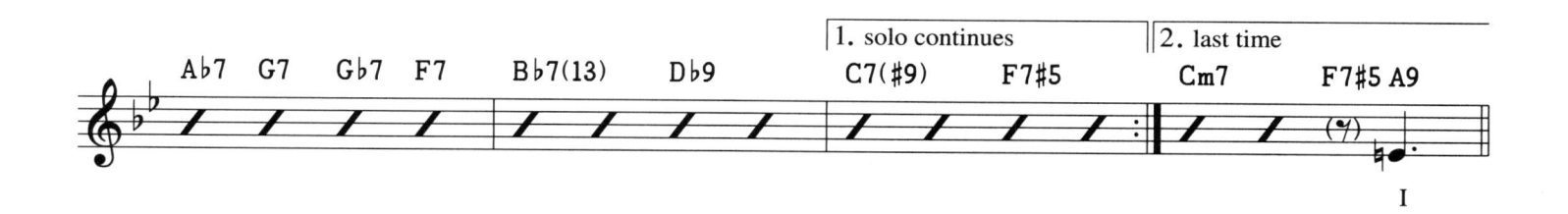

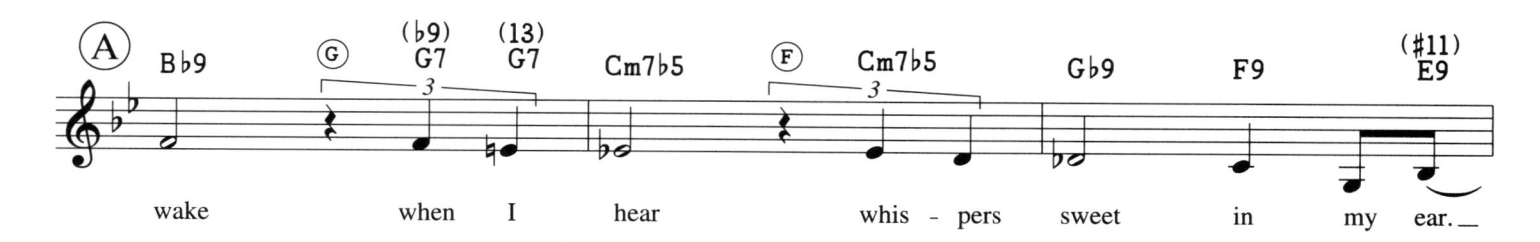

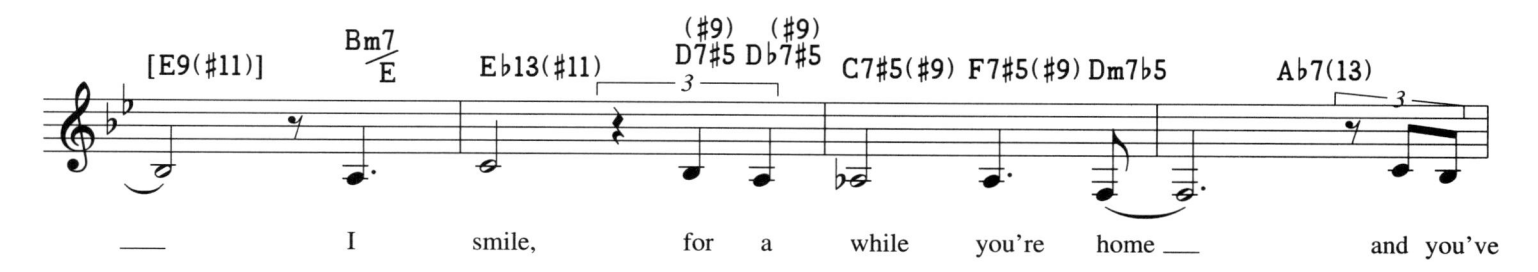

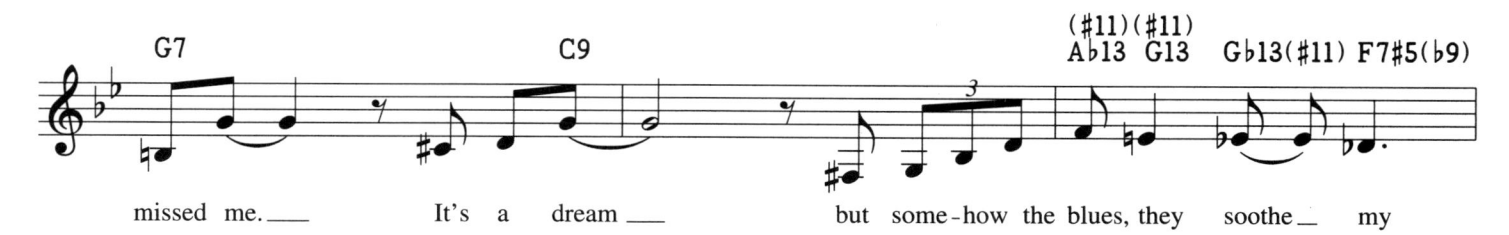

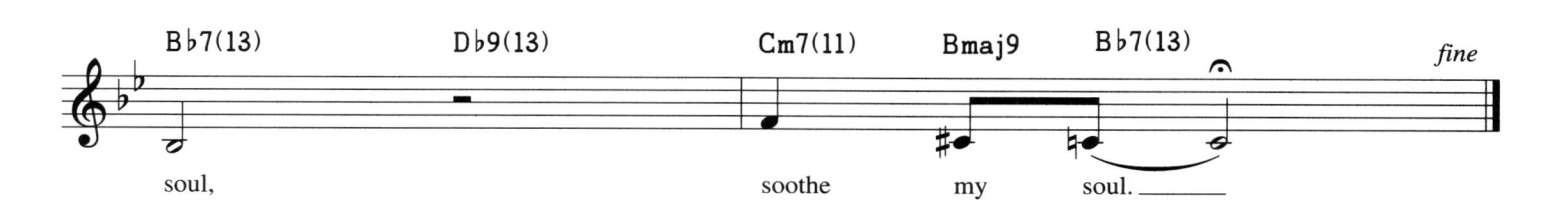

Chapter 12: Chromatic Melody Blues

Solos

Bb7	G7	Cm7b5	F7	Gb7	F7	E9(#11)
	C7(#9)					

Eb7	C7#5(#9) F7#5	Dm7b5 Ab7	G7	C7

Ab7 G7 Gb7 F7	Bb7(13) Db9	*1. solo continues* C7(#9) F7#5	*2. last time* Cm7 F7#5 A9

A

Bb9 — wake

(G) G7(b9) G7(13) — when I

Cm7b5 — hear

(F) Cm7b5 — whis-pers

Gb9 — sweet

F9 — in my

E9(#11) — ear.

[E9(#11)] — I

Bm7/E — smile,

Eb13(#11) — for a

D7#5(#9) Db7#5(#9) — while

C7#5(#9) F7#5(#9) Dm7b5 — you're home

Ab7(13) — and you've

G7 — missed me.

C9 — It's a dream

Ab13(#11) G13(#11) Gb13(#11) F7#5(b9) — but some-how the blues, they soothe my

Bb7(13) — soul,

Db9(13) —

Cm7(11) — soothe

Bmaj9 — my

Bb7(13) — soul.

fine

Chapter 13: Simultaneous Improvising

Over The Brink was originally an instrumental by trombonist Julian Priester, called *Push Come to Shove*. When we recorded this in the studio, I sang the lyric chorus, and Julian and I improvised together, exploring the floating, dreamy mood. I thought we had agreed that I was going to sing one more lyric chorus and finish the song, but Julian and the band played on. You'll hear me finish the lyric, then scat a few phrases before taking it out. After we listened back to the take, we decided we liked the freshness of this "accidental arrangement."

When you're ready to improvise, "mistakes" can provide an opportunity to be creative. So, when you're in the studio recording with your band and something unexpected happens, don't stop the take! Keep on singing: beautiful moments come when you least expect them.

In the accompaniment-only track, there's a solo chorus for you to experiment with before the last melody chorus.

vocal lead sheet
B♭

OVER THE BRINK
Instrumentally known as "Push Come to Shove"

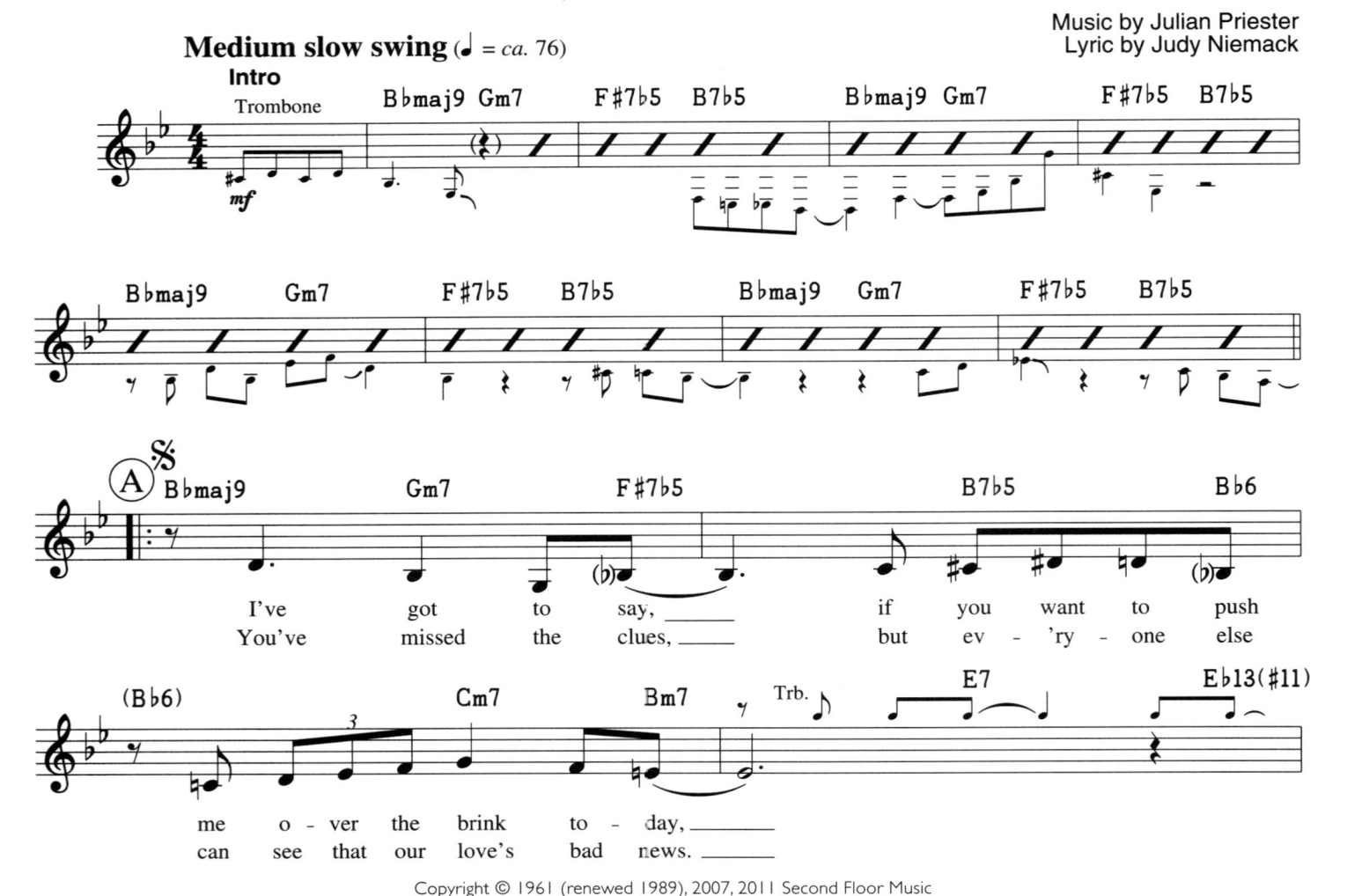

Music by Julian Priester
Lyric by Judy Niemack

Medium slow swing (♩ = ca. 76)

Lyrics:
I've got to say, if you want to push me o - ver the brink to - day,
You've missed the clues, but ev - 'ry - one else can see that our love's bad news.

Copyright © 1961 (renewed 1989), 2007, 2011 Second Floor Music

[E♭13(♯11)]
F♯maj7(♯11)
B7♭5
B♭maj7
keep it up ___ that way ___ and you just
Noth - ing left ___ to lose. ___ Here's a choice
Cm7
Dm7
E♭maj7 G7(♯9)
D♭13(♯11)
C7(♯11)
(♯11)
Bmaj7
might have to pay ___ some ___ dues. ___ You're gon - na lose _
you can't re - fuse: ___ dig ___ in, ___ play it to win _
[Bmaj7(♯11)]
F7(♯9)
B♭maj7
D♭13(♯11)
F♯13(♯11)
B13(♯11)
last time
___ the sweet - est thing you've ev - er ___ dreamed ___ of. ___
___ and get a life, or I'll ___ go ___ my ___ way. ___
Solos
B♭maj9 Gm7 F♯maj7♭5 B7♭5 B♭6 Cm7 Bm7 E7
E♭13(♯11) F♯maj7(♯11) B7♭5 B♭maj7 Cm7 Dm7 E♭maj7 G7♯5 D♭9(♯11)
C9(♯11) B9(♯11) F7♯5(♯9) B♭maj7 D♭7 F♯7 B7
Trb.
D.S. al
Coda
B♭maj9 Gm7 F♯maj7♭5
O - ver the brink. ___

Chapter 14: Voices in Blues

The Birth of the Blues

> *"There was one emotional outlet my people always had when they had the blues. That was singing."*
> — Ethel Waters

The blues were born out of the emotional, spiritual and physical suffering of slaves who could express themselves freely only in song. They show us the inner strength people find when the going gets tough, and how sharing one's troubles somehow lightens the load. Blues developed from field hollers, spirituals and work songs of Southern slaves exploited in plantation cotton fields. They came from the songs of prisoners on chain gangs, laying miles of railroad track in the sun, their grunts and hollers in time with the beating of the hammers on the crossties. The cry of the street vendor, driving through town on his mule-drawn wagon, selling fruits and vegetables and singing out "Watermelon!" or "Cherries, red, ripe cherries!" also found its way into the early blues. These songs consisted of repetitive, chant-like melodies made up of five or six note scales, and included call and response patterns typical of the music of West African tribes that made up almost eighty-five percent of the slaves finally brought to the United States.

> *"The reason for the remarkable development of the rhythmic qualities of African music can certainly be traced to the fact that Africans also used drums for communication; and not, as was once thought, merely by using the drums in a kind of primitive Morse code, but by the phonetic reproduction of the words themselves—the result being that Africans developed an extremely fine and extremely complex rhythmical sense, as well as becoming unusually responsive to timbral subtleties."*
> — Blues People, LeRoi Jones

Blues borrowed European musical elements from ballads, dance tunes and religious songs. After the slaves were freed, they evolved into songs about everyday life. These were occasionally songs of protest, but more often about love, sex, money, travel, hope or despair. Stories of relationships between men and women were often treated with unabashed directness, and tragic and oppressive conditions were faced and defied with courage and humor.

Originally the blues were purely vocal music, but as time passed, black people were able to get or make simple instruments, and by the mid-1800s, they accompanied themselves on harmonica, guitar or banjo. The early blues didn't have a rigid structure; they were improvised according to the whim of the performer, with singing and talking intermingled, and a varying number of measures.

"Blues is truth. Blues are not wrote; the blues are lived."
Brownie McGhee, Blues & Folk singer

The first country blues developed in the rural South, born on the Mississippi Delta. After the Civil War between the Union and Confederacy resulted in the freeing of the slaves in 1865, there was a period of optimism among African-Americans in the South. Slavery was abolished, however this had little effect on their actual living conditions for many years. In 1877, Northern troops withdrew from the South and conditions quickly deteriorated. Many blacks were barred from voting with the imposition of "poll taxes" (fees to be paid in order to vote). The sharecropping system, in which black people rented and farmed land that was owned by white men became the norm. Forced to pay high prices for seed and farm implements, many of them were kept perpetually in debt to their landowners. Justice was scarce, and black people lived in constant fear of lynching. The period from 1890 to 1920 is considered by many historians to be the time of maximum oppression and prejudice against African-Americans, and the blues developed in this atmosphere of extreme suffering, privation and inequality.

Gospel Songs and Hokum Blues

"Blues are the songs of despair, but gospel songs are the songs of hope. "
Mahalia Jackson

When slaves, separated from their native cultures, were converted to Christianity, they integrated their spiritual past wth their newer religious influences. African songs, prayers and chants were transformed into a kind of Christian liturgical music. They embellished the European hymns they sang with blue notes, call and response and other African musical devices, resulting in a new style which later became known as "gospel" music.

In the early days of gospel music, many African-Americans didn't read and there were often no printed hymnals. Call and response was an essential part of the tradition, as the preacher would call out the words for the congregation and they would answer by repeating the last words he said. When the congregation responded, the tempo naturally slowed down at the end of each phrase. Some singers would improvise around the held notes at the end of the phrase, and when one person's melody was especially good, another one might try to top the idea in the next phrase. The congregation encouraged the most spectacular singers, who were believed to be manifesting the Holy Spirit in their singing. The practice of one musician spurring another on to greater heights in a "battle" is a part of both the blues and jazz tradition.

Gospel music was the spiritual counterpart to the secular solo blues. While blues were about hardship and pain, gospel was about religious ecstasy and life after death. And while a good Baptist wouldn't be caught dead singing a low-down dirty blues, church hymns were filled with same rhythmic vitality that inspired the blues. The shouted responses by the congregation and the moans and cries of the blues actually came from the same source: a prayer to God and to man—"Please, hear my cry! Set me free!" By the mid 1890s, newly freed slaves from the Mississippi Delta poured into New Orleans, bringing their songs, the blues, with them.

The blues was strictly a man's music until the early 1900s, sung by itinerant black minstrels and migrant workers who roamed the streets and country roads of the South, looking for work. Minstrel shows were originally performed by whites in "blackface" (which consisted of burnt cork) who imitated and mocked the daily life of a race they deemed inferior in skits and musical numbers. By the end of the Civil War, black people also performed in Negro Minstrel shows, in which they corked their skin and parodied themselves and others. These large touring shows provided the first employment for black entertainers, introducing their music and dances to mass audiences throughout the country.

The Hokum blues style developed out of nineteenth-century Minstrelsy. Hokum was a type of comedic farce, consisting of routines that included monologues, dances, slapstick and music. After the first World War, record companies created a category called "Hokum Blues," which would later include titles like Tampa *Red's Tight Like That,* Robert Johnson's *They're Red Hot,* and *Please Warm My Wiener,* by Bo Carter. These songs, which lampooned both the performers and their audiences, used hilarious analogies or euphemisms referring to all manner of sexual practices and preferences.

Here's an example of hokum lyrics from *Meat Balls,* by Lil Johnson, recorded about 1937:
"Got out late last night, in the rain and sleet
Tryin' to find a butcher that grind my meat
Yes I'm lookin' for a butcher
He must be long and tall
If he want to grind my meat
'Cause I'm wild about my meat balls."

By the 1920s blues singers had moved out of the Southern fields into the cities. When blues recordings were first made in the 1920s, it was the Classic Blues singers, often singing hokum blues, who were the first to be recorded.

Classic Blues and its Stars

Classic blues were composed blues songs with a story line, performed by female singers—professionals—used to singing in front of theater audiences. These women, the first recorded blues singers, were cabaret artists whose backgrounds were far removed from the original folk-blues tradition. Their diction and phrasing owed more to theatrical training than to the folk roots of the blues, and their performances included the trappings of vaudeville: feathers, sequins, pearls and passion.

Gertrude "Ma" Rainey, "The Mother of the Blues," was one of the most imitated and influential of the classic blues singers. Born in 1886, she made her debut at the age of 14 in a local theatre and soon began performing in the Minstrel shows that were popular throughout the South. Ma Rainey was both the first woman to break the tradition of the male blues performer and the first to bring the blues before the footlights. She and her husband "Pa" Rainey, who billed themselves as "assassinators of the blues," performed with various touring companies throughout the South. The Rabbit Foot Minstrels, the most famous of the tent shows, included other blues singers, novelty acts, comedians and vaudeville performers. There were no microphones, and blues singers had to have powerful voices (the term "Blues shouter" originated during this time, for this reason). Her songs were firmly rooted in the folk-blues tradition, and her musicians included the "young lions" of the time, such as Louis Armstrong, who played cornet on her classic blues recording *See, See Rider*.

Up until this time, record companies had assumed that the black population was too poor to afford phonographs or records, and that white consumers would have no interest in black vocal styles. But in 1920, Perry Bradford, an African-American popular and blues songwriter, convinced Okeh Records to record Mamie Smith, making her the first recorded black singer. Although she was far from being an authentic blues singer (her style was more that of the vaudeville tradition), and the title had little relation to the folk-blues roots of the blues, her 78 rpm recording of Bradford's *Crazy Blues* sold a phenomenal 75,000 copies within the first month, starting the blues recording boom. After one year, the company had sold one million copies. Suddenly, other record companies realized that there was a market for "race records" and began recording female blues artists as well. Although Ma Rainey had been touring for some twenty years before Mamie Smith recorded her first record, Ma Rainey's own recording career began at the age of thirty-eight, and she recorded 92 titles from 1923 to 1928. Smith became a major star, and together with Ma Rainey, she established the so-called "classic blues" style. These women performed not only with guitar, but also with a piano or small combo including banjo, clarinet or cornet (like in vaudeville or cabaret shows).

But the woman who stands out as having created the legendary status of the female blues singer was Bessie Smith, the "Empress of the Blues," and one of Billie Holiday's idols. Born in 1898, she was a street singer at the age of 9, and as a teenager was taken under the wing of Ma Rainey, appearing with Rainey in her traveling "Medicine and Minstrels" shows between 1914 and 1916. Eight years older than Bessie Smith, Rainey was a mentor to Bessie, working with her in several touring companies.

If Ma Rainey's style was based in the folk-blues tradition, Bessie Smith's style combined both blues and cabaret music. Her first recording, Alberta Hunter's *Downhearted Blues*, sold 780,000 copies in the first six months. Although she only made $125 for it herself, she became a vaudeville star, and eventually, the highest paid black entertainer of the twenties. Her enormous voice and excellent diction appealed to black and white audiences alike, and she had devoted fans in the upper-crust New York social circles who attended her shows and invited her to their parties. With a huge appetite for pleasure of all kinds, she led a tumultuous life filled with passion and violence. Her lyrics were often laced with double meanings and erotic connotations. Her powerful sound and emotional intensity come across clearly on her records and in her film "St. Louis Blues," despite the limitations of the recording techniques of her time. In the film she plays herself—a blues singer who is caught in a chaotic relationship with a heartless gambler who cheats on her. She sings *St. Louis Blues* while drinking her sorrows away at a bar filled with people who listen sympathetically and then join in, singing a rousing chorus to her tale of woe.

These blues were delivered with great expression and emotion, in a more sophisticated style—closer to jazz. Jazzmen, in fact, were often the sidemen on these recording sessions. Louis Armstrong, Coleman Hawkins and Fletcher Henderson recorded with Ma Rainey, and Armstrong and Henderson were also featured in Bessie Smith's recordings. In the process of creating a new vocabulary, these jazz instrumentalists imitated vocal blues nuances in their playing.

The Father of the Blues

"The blues come from nothingness, from want, from desire..."
W.C. Handy

It wasn't until the turn of the century and the publication of blues as sheet music that the blues settled into a structured form. *Dallas Blues*, published in 1912 by a white violinist named Hart Wand, was the first real blues song to be published. It was played on steamboats the length of the Mississippi River, influencing the sound of blues to come.

However, the man who took the blues and made his name and career out of it was William Christopher Handy. W.C. Handy (1873–1958) came from a line of Baptist ministers in Alabama. He was a black cornetist, bandleader, arranger and music teacher. In 1903, while waiting on a platform in a Mississippi train station, he heard a man playing guitar with a knife (the early version of slide guitar) and singing a song unlike anything he had ever heard. He was deeply impressed, and asked the man what he was playing. "The Blues!" was the reply.

Soon after, while performing with his orchestra for a white people's dance, he was asked by the audience to give the local band a chance to play. A motley group of three instrumentalists played a blues, "one of those over-and-over strains that seemed to have no very clear beginning, and certainly no ending at all." Handy was amazed at the audience response, saying, "a rain of silver dollars began to fall … and there, before those boys lay more money than my nine musicians were being paid for the entire evening!" He concluded: "They had the stuff the people wanted!" Realizing that this music could bring him both income and popularity, he decided to write a blues of his own. His first "blues," a cross-over between ragtime and blues, was a campaign song for a Memphis mayoral candidate. *Mr. Crump* was later renamed *Memphis Blues (A Southern Rag)* and published in 1912. Morton Harvey, a white musician, made it the first blues to be recorded.

In his long and prolific career, Handy's signature work was the *St. Louis Blues,* a fusion of blues with ragtime and jazz, using the Latin Habañera rhythm that had long been a part of ragtime. In 1914, W. C. Handy brought the blues to a certain New York City street, changing the sound of American popular music forever. "Tin Pan Alley," located on 28th Street between Fifth and Sixth Avenues, was the hub of music publishing in the United States. Although Tin Pan Alley publishers rejected his *St. Louis Blues,* it was performed by major singers of the day. Handy decided to publish it himself, which he did with great success. It had an immediate impact on the white musical establishment, and by 1917, blues began to emanate from the top song writing teams of Tin Pan Alley. His success inspired countless others to write blues songs. Handy went on to become a very popular composer, and billed himself as the "Father of the Blues."

The blues waned in popularity in the late 1920s, with the crumbling of the vaudeville and theatrical circuit and the decreased purchasing power of black audiences caused by the Depression. "Nobody wants to hear blues no more," Bessie Smith said. "Times is hard." But along with the development of swing and big-band music in the late 1930s, the blues was revived with the Boogie Woogie piano craze and the discovery of its blues roots, as well as the development of Kansas City big-band blues.

Country Blues and its Stars

"Classic blues was entertainment, and country blues, folk-lore."
LeRoi Jones, "Blues People"

With the success of the female blues singers, record companies became interested in seeking out folk or country singers, and with modern recording technology, a new breed of collectors traveled to various cities to record local artists. Musicologists John and Alan Lomax recorded thousands of songs on portable recording equipment for the Library of Congress. These country blues recordings consisted of men accompanying themselves on acoustic guitar or banjo. The first recordings were made between 1920 and 1940 by such singers as "Blind Lemon" Jefferson and Huddie "Leadbelly" Ledbetter.

"Blind Lemon" Jefferson (1893-1929) was the first folk blues "star" and a founder of the Texas blues sound, which featured swing rhythm and single-line guitar solos. One of the most popular and influential blues singers of the 1920s, he had a fast, intricate style of guitar playing and a high-pitched voice. Many of his songs were covered by other musicians, including *See That My Grave Is Kept Clean*, recorded by Bob Dylan, and *Matchbox Blues*, recorded by The Beatles more than 30 years after the original. He is said to have musically influenced such jazz artists as Louis Armstrong, Bessie Smith and Bix Beiderbecke.

"The blues is a feeling and when it hits you, it's the real news."
Huddie "Leadbelly" Ledbetter

Huddie Ledbetter, or "Leadbelly" (1888-1949) was called "King of the twelve-string guitar" and had a repertoire of some 500 songs. A companion of Blind Lemon, he became a long-time inmate of Southern penitentiaries, and later the darling of the white East Coast liberal establishment. He was a raconteur, womanizer, brawler, braggart and in latter days a devotee of left-wing causes. He had a unique way of combining storytelling with singing, using accompanied spoken introductions to his songs (some of which were as long as the song itself).

Big Bill Broonzy (1898-1958) was one of the most famous country blues singers, in a style called Delta Blues, a form characterized by fiery "bottleneck" or slide guitar and passionate lyrics. He recorded 260 songs from 1925 to 1952, and was the first blues artist to tour Europe and South Africa, and later to play at Carnegie Hall. Due to his discovery by John Hammond (who was actually looking for Robert Johnson to perform in his "Spirituals to Swing" concert at Carnegie Hall), Broonzy became famous during the 1960s folk and blues revival, and later was an inspiration for British guitarist Eric Clapton.

> *"Blues is a natural fact, is something that a fellow lives. If you don't live it, you don't have it.... Young people have forgotten to cry the blues. Now they talk and get lawyers and things."* — Big Bill Broonzy

During the 1930s, blues music underwent a broad transformation, and female vocalists like Bessie Smith found themselves out of work as male guitarists like Big Bill Broonzy and Tampa Red captured the record-buying public's taste. One woman, Memphis Minnie (1897-1973), transcended this change with her powerful vocals and six-string guitar skills that rivaled and, in many cases, surpassed those of her male contemporaries.

Born Lizzie Douglas, as a teenager Minnie played banjo and guitar for tips in the streets of Memphis. By the 1920s, she was established in the Beale Street blues scene. Columbia Records discovered her and released *Bumble Bee,* her first recording as Memphis Minnie, in 1929. The song financed a move to Chicago, which furthered her career. Although she wore expensive dresses and a bracelet made of silver dollars, Minnie had come up in the rough, tough juke joints of the South, and wasn't afraid of a fight. She won a guitar battle with two of Chicago's reigning blues giants, Big Bill Broonzy and Tampa Red, earning her the respect of both, and recorded almost 200 sides during the 1930s and '40s. Minnie was one of the first blues artists to play an electric guitar, and her fusion of country and urban blues paved the way for artists like Muddy Waters and Bo Diddley.

The Piedmont blues style originated on the East Coast. During the Great Migration, many black Americans moved to this region, and hemmed in by the Appalachian Mountains to the west, bluesmen who might otherwise have settled in rural areas stayed in cities, where they were exposed to a wider variety of musical styles. Unlike the blues of the Mississippi delta, Piedmont blues were influenced by ragtime, country, and popular songs, and characterized by fast finger-picking on the guitar. Blind Blake, Blind Boy Fuller, Rev. Gary Davis, and Barbecue Bob are among the most influential of the Piedmont style bluesmen, but perhaps the best-known was the duo of harmonica player Sonny Terry and guitarist Brownie McGhee, each of whom had careers that stretched from the 1930s into the '90s.

Blind Boy Fuller (1908-1941) had an expressive voice and an impressive finger-picking guitar style. Born in North Carolina, he learned the traditional field hollers and country rags from older singers. During his late teens, he lost his sight, and turned to playing on street corners and in front of tobacco warehouses. Between 1935 and 1940, Fuller recorded over 120 songs, many of which have become blues standards. His repertoire ranged from ragtime to hokum blues, including such titles as *Truckin' My Blues Away* and *I Want Some Of Your Pie.* In other songs, like *Pistol Slapper Blues,* he drew upon his experience as an underprivileged, blind black man living on the streets in the South, writing lyrics about poverty, violence and death.

Robert Johnson (1911-1938) was the most influential Delta Blues singer and guitarist. His famous song *Crossroads* tells of his midnight meeting with the devil at a crossroads, where he sells his soul in return for superhuman musical powers on the guitar. Johnson died young, ostensibly poisoned with strychnine-laced whiskey by the jealous husband of a woman he'd flirted with at a party. Unfortunately, this was shortly before either the Lomaxes or jazz and blues promoter John Hammond could find him and bring him to New York. Although he recorded only 29 selections in his two year recording period, Johnson became famous posthumously due to the release of *King of the Delta Blues* in 1961, which had a direct influence on British rock musicians who later covered his songs, including Led Zeppelin, Cream, The Rolling Stones, The Red Hot Chili Peppers and others.

Urban Blues

> *"Jazz is the big brother of the blues. If a guy's playing blues like we play, he's in high school. When he starts playing jazz it's like going on to college, to a school of higher learning."*   B. B. King

In the 1940s a new blues style evolved, later called "urban blues." Blues became electrified with the introduction of the amplified guitar, and musicians began using instruments like bass, drums and brass. In Northern cities like Chicago and Detroit, Muddy Waters, Willie Dixon, John Lee Hooker, Howlin' Wolf, and Elmore James played what was basically Mississippi Delta blues, backed by bass, drums, piano and occasionally harmonica, and began having national hits with blues songs.

At the same time in Los Angeles, Texas blues guitarist and singer Aaron Thibeaux ("T-Bone") Walker (1910-1974) began to use jazz accompanists on his gigs. His *Stormy Monday* (recorded in 1946) became a blues standard. T-Bone was of Cherokee Indian decent. He was the first to use the guitar to play melodic phrases like a horn player, and played the blues with a new sense of sophistication and technical brilliance. His West Coast style influenced B.B. King, who said that hearing *Stormy Monday* inspired him to play electric guitar. Both T-Bone Walker and B.B. King pioneered a style of guitar playing that combined jazz technique with the blues tonality and repertoire.

Born near Clarksdale, Mississippi, to a sharecropper family, John Lee Hooker (1917-2001) was one of the last links to the blues of the Deep South. He moved to Detroit in the early 1940s and developed the half-spoken singing style that became his trademark. By 1948, he had his first jukebox hit and million-seller, *Boogie Chillun.*

In the late 1940s, Chicago was the pivotal locale for the development of the modern blues. The revolution began in 1948 with the release of a 78 rpm single by singer-guitarist

Muddy Waters (1915-1983) with two traditional Mississippi Delta-styled songs, *I Can't Be Satisfied* and *I Feel Like Going Home*. His later hits included *She's Nineteen Years Old, Walking Through the Park, You Can't Lose What You Ain't Never Had,* and the classic, *Got My Mojo Working*. Influenced by Son House and Robert Johnson, he used the guitar as an extension of his voice, the sliding bottleneck matching the dips, slurs and sliding notes of his singing. He began performing on the "chitlin' circuit." "Chitlins" are a soul-food dish made from boiled pig intestines, called "chitterlings," and the "chitlin' circuit" was the name given to the string of performance venues that ran through the eastern and southern United States. These venues were safe performance spaces for black musicians during an age of racial segregation.

As the '50s gave way to the '60s and to the full force of the Civil Rights Movement, blues of the sort Waters performed became less relevant to black listeners who wanted to leave behind the memory of slavery and the Mississippi Delta sound. Soul music, the blues styles of B.B. King and modern black dance music became more popular. But Waters and other blues performers of his generation were discovered and taken up by a young, white and middle-class audience that had been born of the folk music revival of the late 1950s—an audience that grew considerably a few years later with the British blues boom. The bars, taverns and dancehalls of the "chitlin' circuit" were replaced by college auditoriums, festival stages, folksong, blues and jazz clubs. International tours and television appearances fostered a wide acceptance of blues artists by the rock community. The Rolling Stones actually took their name from a line in one of Waters' songs, and many other British rock bands covered his tunes or songs he recorded as well.

Memphis Blues singer Riley "B.B." King ("Blues Boy King") used jazz musicians to back him up for 35 years. Soon after his number one hit, *Three O'Clock Blues,* B.B. began touring nationally. In 1956, he and his band played 342 one-night stands. Over the years, B.B. developed one of the world's most identifiable guitar styles. He borrowed from Charlie Christian, Blind Lemon Jefferson, "T-Bone" Walker and others, integrating complex vocal-like string bends and a left hand vibrato, both of which have become indispensable components of rock guitarists' vocabulary. Mixing traditional blues, jazz, swing, mainstream pop and jump into a unique sound, he has been a model for players from Eric Clapton and George Harrison to Jeff Beck. B.B.King's career has spanned fifty years, and to this day he continues to sing, play and record. One of the greatest blues singers and guitarists of all time, the "King of the Blues" and his guitar "Lucille" influenced generations of guitarists and helped give the blues its special place in the American musical tradition.

George "Buddy" Guy (1936-) is considered by many musicians to be the last urban "blueser." Known as an inspiration to Jimi Hendrix, Eric Clapton, Led Zepplin and Stevie Ray Vaughan, Guy is an important exponent of Chicago blues. He is known for his showmanship, playing his guitar with drumsticks, pulling someone up from the audience to strum while he plays the chords, or strolling into the audience, jamming and trailing a long guitar chord. While his music is often labeled Chicago blues, his style is unique, varying from traditional blues to a creative, unpredictable mixture of the blues, avant rock, soul and free jazz that comes out differently every night.

Jump and Jive

Jazz began to shape the blues in the 1940s with the beginning of the rhythm and blues style called "jive" or "jump" blues. Louis Jordan's "Tympany Five" was one of the most influential of the jump music groups, and was tremendously popular in Harlem. By 1942 they were one of the most popular recording acts in the country. They combined Count Basie-style riffs with a boogie-based shuffle, and hits such as *Ain't Nobody Here But Us Chickens* and *Choo Choo Ch'Boogie* inspired countless "jump blues" combos.

Though largely retaining the sound and subject matter of his African-American roots, Jordan enjoyed celebrity status among both blacks and whites, starring in numerous Hollywood short films and receiving equal billing on recordings with Louis Armstrong and Bing Crosby. *I'm Gonna Move on the Outskirts of Town, Let the Good Times Roll, Caldonia, Ain't That Just Like a Woman, What's the Use of Getting Sober* and *Saturday Night Fish Fry* are some of his many hits. The bouncing, rhythmic vitality of his music, coupled with clever lyrics and an engaging stage presence, enabled Jordan to become one of the few black artists of the 1940s to enjoy crossover popularity with a white audience. His musical style exerted a profound influence on a wide range of performers, most notably Chuck Berry, Ray Charles, Bill Haley, Woody Herman, Muddy Waters, and Eric Clapton.

Blues in Jazz

> *"Blues is like the folk themes and little nuggets and kernels that are developed through the art of jazz into jazz music. You have to have that blues. Blues is like the roux in a gumbo. Now you might have a soup, and it might be killin', but if you don't have that roux, you cannot have no gumbo. People always ask me if jazz has the blues in it. I say, if it sounds good it does."*   An Interview with Wynton Marsalis
> "Jazz, a History of America's Music," Geoffrey C. Ward and Ken Burns

The blues are one of the most important roots of jazz music and to this day serve as an essential part of the jazz repertoire.

During the thirties and forties, the blues spread northward with the migration of Southern black people in search of jobs, entering into the repertoire of big-band jazz. Jimmy Rushing (1901-1972) was born in Okalahoma, but made his name in Kansas City. Affectionately called "Mr. Five By Five," due to his short height and large girth, he was one of the first blues-based singers to front a big band. In 1927, he joined Walter Page's Blue Devils in Kansas City, and then joined Bennie Moten's band in 1929. He stayed with Moten's successor, Count Basie, when Moten died in 1935, and became famous singing with the Count Basie Orchestra from 1935 to 1950. He had a clear, nasal tenor voice that dominated the band even without a microphone. His vocal style was that of the "blues shouter," which was developed to its fullest in the 1940s by singers with the Kansas City swing bands, including Big Joe Turner, Jimmy Witherspoon and Walter Brown.

> *"There were no microphones in those days, and unless you could overshadow the horns they wouldn't let you sing. You had to have a good pair of lungs.. (strong!) to reach out over the band and the people in those big dance halls."*
>   Jimmy Rushing

Jimmy Rushing's blues, *Going to Chicago*, was a hit when his recording with the Count Basie Band was released in the late '30s, and interpretations continue to be recorded to this day. In 1958, Jon Hendricks wrote vocalese lyrics to the entire big band arrangement, recorded it with his vocal trio, Lambert, Hendricks and Ross, on an album entitled "Sing Along With Basie." This album featured Basie's vocalist Joe Williams and the Count Basie Orchestra. In 1962, Mark Murphy recorded it again, singing the entire arrangement by himself ("Mark Murphy: That's How I Love the Blues")! One of the most recent recordings is a live performance by Kurt Elling with guest Jon Hendricks at Chicago's Green Mill jazz club, a tour de force by two jazz greats. If you start with Jimmy Rushing's version and listen to each one, you'll hear the transformation of a simple blues into an entire story, interpreted in four quite different ways.

Oran "Hot Lips" Page (1908-1954), born in Dallas, Texas, was a jazz trumpeter, blues shouter and bandleader—a scorching soloist and a powerful vocalist. He backed such blues singers as Ma Rainey, Bessie Smith and Ida Cox, and played with bands including the legendary Blue Devils and Count Basie's original Reno Club Orchestra.

Mildred Bailey (1903-1951) was a popular jazz singer of the 1930s. The Native American woman sang in the Paul Whiteman Orchestra. She had a light, clear, bell-like voice and a musician's ear, with a style that bridged the gap between jazz and the commercial music of her time. Later she often performed with her husband, vibraphonist Red Norvo. Together they were known as "Mr. And Mrs. Swing." Check out her recording of *St. Louis Blues* to hear a swing treatment of this classic.

> *"Of course, there are a lot of ways you can treat the blues, but it will still be the blues."* — Count Basie

After World War II, the influence of blues on jazz remained, and many of the bebop classics are based on the use of the pentatonic and blues scale over various blues progressions. During the Bebop era, there was a major shift of jazz from pop music for dancing to a less accessible, more cerebral "musician's music." The audience for blues and jazz split, definitively marking the border between the two musical genres.

> *"Billie Holiday's voice was the voice of living intensity of soul in the true sense of that greatly abused word. As a human being she was sweet, sour, kind, mean, generous, profane, lovable and impossible, and nobody who knew her expects to see anyone quite like her again."* — Leonard Feather

Billie Holiday (1915-1959) rarely sang blues, and did not consider herself to be a blues singer, although many people still attach this label to her name. Perhaps this common misconception is due to her phrasing, bending of notes and the crying timbre that infuses her versions of Tin Pan Alley songs. She sang the occasional blues (*Billie's Blues, Now or Never, Fine and Mellow,* and *Baby Get Lost*) with her signature style: laid back and sultry. In any case, she embodied the melancholy mood so often associated with the word "blues."

Joe Williams (1918-1999) sang with the Count Basie Band from 1954 to 1961, where his fame was established with the hit recording of *Every Day I Have the Blues.* Another Basie hit was *Alright, OK, You Win* which, in my opinion, is the quintessence of swing. Joe had a rich bass-baritone voice, with a relaxed, deeply swinging style, and occasionally incorporated yodeling techniques into his vocals.

> *"You can't separate modern jazz from rock or from rhythm and blues—you can't separate it. Because that's where it all started, and that's where it all come from—that's where I learned to keep rhythm—in church."* — Art Blakey

Dinah Washington (1924-1963), "The Queen of Blues," started as a gospel singer and had her first blues hits in 1943. She was successful as a singer of classic blues, raunchy rhythm and blues, jazz, country and pop songs throughout the '50s and up until her early death. She recorded several blues penned by jazz critic Leonard Feather, including *Long John Blues*, which tells the story of her visit to her dentist, Long John, who "thrills me when he drills me," among other evocative images. One can hear echoes of Dinah in the phrasing of jazz vocalists Nancy Wilson and Little Jimmy Scott. Her penetrating sound, solid time, and crystal-clear enunciation bring a distinctive flavor to every song she recorded. While making great recordings in jazz, blues, R&B and pop genres, she never recorded gospel music because she believed that it was wrong to mix the secular and spiritual. Once she had entered the secular music world professionally, she refused to include gospel in her repertoire. With her biggest hit, *What a Diff'rence a Day Makes,* she won a Grammy in 1959 for the Best Rhythm and Blues Song.

> *"All the classic jazz players sang and a lot of 'em sang blues."* Mose Allison

Mose Allison, the "Sage of Tippo," was born in 1927 on his grandfather's farm in Tippo, a cotton town in the Mississippi Delta. His songs are a fusion of rustic blues and jazz, with profound and often humorous lyrics. He blends the raw blues of his childhood with the modern pianistic influences of John Lewis and Thelonious Monk. His songs have been covered by Van Morrison, The Clash, Eric Clapton, the Yardbirds, Elvis Costello and Bonnie Raitt, and his music has influenced blues and rock artists including The Rolling Stones, John Mayall and The Who, who played his song *Young Man Blues* on several tours.

Since their invention, blues have been adopted by scores of different races and nationalities, spawning musical styles like jazz, rhythm and blues, rock 'n' roll, soul, funk and hip-hop. The term "blues" covers a wide variety of styles, from Robert Johnson's one-man version of *Crossroads* to Joe Williams' *Every Day* with the Count Basie Orchestra, from Billie Holiday's laid-back *Fine and Mellow* to Janis Joplin's screaming *Ball and Chain.* Blues have traveled a long way from their early origins and continue to evolve today. I hope this brief introduction will ignite your interest in exploring the history of this wonderful music through the resources listed in the appendix.

Appendix

"The blues, they feel good. The blues is many things: a philosophy and a form, a musical form of bars and measures, a whole body of melodies and themes. It's a harmonic system. It's a system of call and response. It's a bunch of moans and groans and shouts and cries. Dissonance and consonance. Blues is many things. And it can interface with music all over the world."

An Interview with Wynton Marsalis from "Jazz, a History of America's Music," Geoffrey C. Ward and Ken Burns

What are blues? The Miriam Webster Dictionary defines blues as "noun plural but singular or plural in construction (1) low spirits: melancholy, "suffering a case of the blues," (2) a song often of lamentation characterized by usually 12-bar phrases, 3-line stanzas in which the words of the second line usually repeat those of the first, and continual occurrence of blue notes in melody and harmony, and (3) jazz or popular music using harmonic and phrase structures of blues." The etymology of the word dates all the way back to 1741, when sad or melancholy feelings were called "blue devils," and according to Webster, an early reference to "the blues" can be found in 1798, in George Colman's "Blue devils, a farce in one act."

Listen and Learn

Blues were originally passed down by ear. They evolved in performance; each singer had their own way of phrasing; they varied melodies and even the words. Luckily there are many recordings available of blues performers, as well as live concerts in most major cities. Take advantage of the opportunity to listen to the originals. No matter how clearly a song is written down or how well someone describes a blues singer, there's no substitute for hearing the music.

Imitation is a traditional part of singing the blues. When you've found a recording of a blues singer you like, listen to it until it starts to become familiar and then sing along. Don't try to copy the singer's tone quality; that could lead to vocal problems. Focus on the melody and the phrasing, using your own sound. Practice until you can match the notes and timing, then try singing it without the recording. Eventually your own interpretation will evolve.

By the way, blues lyrics sometimes include slang words that are puzzling to the modern listener. For example, Ma Rainey's *See, See Rider* has several explanations. Some say it's about the County Circuit Riders, or C.C. Riders, the preachers who traveled on horseback, came into town for a night and left the next day for the next town—and the next woman. Another explanation is that during the Great Depression of the late 1920s and early 1930s, poor people hitched rides on the trains that crisscrossed the country. One slow train, the Colorado Central, had the initials C.C., and a "C.C. Rider" might have been a traveling man. Sexual innuendos in blues are common, and an "easy rider" could also refer to a prostitute.

So, whenever possible, know what you're singing about—*Wild About that Jelly Roll* is not an ode to pastry and *I'm Gonna Dust my Broom* is not about cleaning house!

Essential Listening

Blues Pioneers
- Big Bill Broonzy "Good Time Tonight" (1990, Sony)
- Blind Boy Fuller "Blind Boy Fuller" Remastered 1935-1938 (JSP Records, 2004)
- Blind Lemon Jefferson "King of the Country Blues" (Yazoo)

Classic Blues
- Alberta Hunter "Down-Hearted Blues" (2001, Varese Sarabande)
- Ma Rainey "Ma Rainey" (1992, Milestone)
- Bessie Smith "The Essential Bessie Smith" (1997, Alligator Records)
- Mamie Smith "Crazy Blues, the Best of Mamie Smith" (2004, Sony)

Delta Blues
- Son House "The Original Delta Blues" (1998, Sony)
- Robert Johnson "The Complete Recordings" (1990, Sony)
- Muddy Waters "Folk Singer" (1999, Chess)

Texas Blues
- Sam Lightnin' Hopkins "Texas Blues" (1990, Arhoolie Records)
- Huddy Leadbelly Ledbetter "Alabama Bound" (1990, RCA)
- T-Bone Walker "T-Bone Blues" (1990, Atlantic/WEA)

Chicago Blues
- Memphis Minnie "Queen of Blues" (Sony, 1997)
- Elmore James "Guitars in Orbit" (Collectibles, 1998)
- Muddy Waters "Chess Box" (1999, Chess Records)
- Howlin' Wolf "The Real Folk Blues" (Chess/MCA)

Urban Blues
- Buddy Guy "This is Buddy Guy!" (1989, MCA)
- John Lee Hooker "The Very Best of John Lee Hooker" (1995, Rhino/WEA)
- B.B. King "Live at the Regal" (1965, MCA)

Jump and Jive
- Louis Jordan "Saturday Night Fish Fry" (2001, Jasmine Music)

Blues Shouters
- Jimmy Rushing "Going to Chicago" (1994, Blues Forever)
- Big Joe Turner "Big Joe Turner's Greatest Hits" (1990, Atlantic)

Rhythm and Blues
- Ruth Brown "Miss Rhythm, Greatest Hits and More" (1989, Atlantic/WEA)
- Etta James "Blues to the Bone" (2004, RCA Victor)
- Dinah Washington "Jazz Masters 19" (1994, Polygram Records)

Blues in Jazz
- Mose Allison "Your Mind Is on Vacation" (1990, Atlantic/WEA)
- Karrin Allyson "In Blue" (2004, Concord Records)
- Peggy Lee "Blues Cross Country" (1991, EMI Int'l)
- Kevin Mahogany "Big Band" (2005, Lightyear)
- Mark Murphy "That's How I Love the Blues" (1962, OJC)
- Catherine Russell "Sentimental Streak" (2008, Harmonium Mundi/World Village)
- Joe Williams "Everyday I Have the Blues" (2007, CFP)

Modern Female Favorites:
- Janis Joplin "Greatest Hits" (1999, Sony)
- Bonnie Raitt "The Bonnie Raitt Collection" (1995, WEA)
- Koko Taylor "Queen of the Blues" (1990, Alligator Records)

Blues at a Jam Session

Blues are often the first thing jazz musicians will play at a jam session, since most instrumentalists are familiar with the chord progression. The following 12-bar instrumental blues are often played. If you learn to scat a few of these blues "heads" (melodies) you'll be able to join in.

Au Privave (Charlie Parker)
Bag's Groove Milt Jackson
Barbados (Charlie Parker)
Billie's Bounce (Charlie Parker)
Blue Monk (Thelonious Monk)
Blue Train (John Coltrane)
Blues For Alice (Charlie Parker)
Blues in the Closet (Oscar Pettiford)
C Jam Blues (Duke Ellington)
Cheryl (Charlie Parker)
Equinox (John Coltrane)
Footprints (Wayne Shorter) [3/4, minor blues]
Now's the Time (Charlie Parker)
Straight, No Chaser (Thelonious Monk)
Things Ain't What They Used to Be (Duke Ellington)
Turnaround (Ornette Coleman)

Blues with Lyrics

Here are some of my favorite blues with lyrics. These titles work well in a jazz set.
All Blues (Miles Davis, Oscar Brown, Jr.)
Alright, O.K., You Win (Sid Wyche, Mayme Watts)
Ancient Footprints (Wayne Shorter, Kitty Margolis) [instrumentally *Footprints*]

Billie's Blues (Billie Holiday)

Blues in the Night (Harold Arlen, Johnny Mercer)

Bluesette (Jean "Toots" Thielemans, Norman Gimbel)

Chillin' (Paul Chambers, R. Rachel Mackin) [instrumentally *Whims of Chambers*]

A Crazy Song to Sing (Thelonious Monk, Judy Niemack) [instrumentally *Misterioso*]

Centerpiece (Harry "Sweets" Edison, Jon Hendricks)

Comin' Home Baby (Bob Dorough, Ben Tucker)

Doodlin' (Horace Silver)

Dry Cleaner From Des Moines (Charles Mingus, Joni Mitchell)

Everyday I Have the Blues (Peter Chapman)

Fine and Mellow (Billie Holiday)

Gambler's Blues (Dinah Washington)

Get It Straight (Thelonious Monk, Sally Swisher) [instrumentally *Straight, No Chaser*]

Goodbye Pork Pie Hat (Charles Mingus, Joni Mitchell)

I'm a Woman (Ellis McDaniel, Koko Taylor)

I'm Gonna Move to the Outskirts of Town (William Weldon, Roy Jordan)

Interplay (Bill Evans, Judy Niemack)

Kansas City (Jerry Lieber, Mike Stoller, Richard Penniman)

Long John Blues (Dinah Washington)

A Long Way to Go (John Coltrane, Karrin Allyson) (instrumentally *Equinox*)

Mad about Him, Sad without Him, How Can I Be Glad without Him Blues (L. Marks, D. Charles)

Monkery's the Blues (Thelonious Monk, Abbey Lincoln) [instrumentally *Blue Monk*]

My Little Sherri (Charlie Rouse, Ben Sidran) [instrumentally *Little Sherri*]

Oh! Gee! (Matthew Gee)

Red Top (Lionel Hampton, Ben Kynard)

Roll 'em Pete (Pete Johnson, Joe Turner)

Route 66 (Bobby Troup)

Sassy's Blues (Sarah Vaughan, Thad Jones)

See, See Rider (Ma Rainey)

Señor Blues (Horace Silver)

Soft Winds (Fletcher Henderson, Fred Royal)

St. Louis Blues (W.C. Handy)

Stolen Moments (Oliver Nelson, Mark Murphy)

Stormy Monday (T-Bone Walker)

Strollin' (Charles Mingus)

There's No More Blue Time (Tadd Dameron, Georgie Fame) [instrumentally *A Blue Time*]

T.V. Blues (Bob Mintzer)

Your Mind Is on Vacation (Mose Allison)

Riff Blues

These titles can be performed either as melodies or as "riffs" behind a soloist on the blues. You can even combine them and sing several at the same time in a vocal ensemble.

Bag's Groove (Milt Jackson)
Birth of a Band (Quincy Jones)
Bluebird (Charlie Parker)
Blues Backstage (Frank Foster)
Blues in the Closet (Oscar Pettiford)
Bud's Blues (Bud Powell)
C Jam Blues (Duke Ellington)
Centerpiece (Harry "Sweets" Edison)
Cool Blues (Charlie Parker)
Emanon (Dizzy Gillespie)
Night Train (Jimmy Forrest, Oscar Washington)
One O'Clock Jump (Count Basie)
Sack O' Woe (Julian "Cannonball" Adderly)
Sonnymoon for Two (Sonny Rollins)
Swingin' the Blues (Eddie Durham, Count Basie)
That's What I'm Talkin' 'Bout (Shorty Rogers)

Vocalese Blues

Each of these songs was originally an instrumental recording with an improvised solo to which lyrics were added later.

Billie's Bounce (Charlie Parker, Eddie Jefferson)
Doodlin' (Horace Silver, Jon Hendricks)
Farmer's Market (Art Farmer, Annie Ross)
Freddie Freeloader (Miles Davis, Jon Hendricks)
Goin' to Chicago (Jimmy Rushing, Jon Hendricks)
Goodbye Pork Pie Hat (Charles Mingus, Joni Mitchell)
Jackie (Hampton Hawes, Annie Ross)
Little Boy, Don't Get Scared (Stan Getz, King Pleasure)
McSplivins (Dexter Gordon, Judy Niemack)
Now's the Time (Charlie Parker, Eddie Jefferson)
Parker's Mood (Charlie Parker, King Pleasure)
Run Home (Dexter Gordon, Judy Niemack)
Twisted (Wardell Grey, Annie Ross)

Resources and recommended reading

Albertson, Chris. "Bessie" Yale University Press; Rev Exp edition, 2003

Bogdanov, Vladimir, et al. "The All Music Guide to the Blues: The Definitive Guide to the Blues"

Clarke, Donald. "Wishing on the Moon: The Life and Times of Billie Holiday" Da Capo Press, 2002

Davis, Francis. "The History Of The Blues: The Roots, The Music, The People" Da Capo Press, 2003

Davis, Angela Yvonne. "Blues Legacies and Black Feminism: Gertrude 'Ma' Rainey, Bessie Smith and Billie Holiday" Vintage; 1st Vintage Books Edition, 1999

Dufty, William and Billie Holiday. "Lady Sings the Blues" Harlem Moon, 50 Anv. Edition, 2006

Guralnick, Peter, et al. "Martin Scorsese Presents The Blues: A Musical Journey" 2003

Jones, LeRoi. "Blues People: Negro Music in White America", William Morrow & Company, 1999

Oliver, Paul. "The Story of the Blues" Northeastern, 1998

Oliver, Paul. "Blues Fell this Morning: Meaning in the Blues" Cambridge University Press; 2nd edition, 1990

Russell, Tony. "The Blues: From Robert Johnson to Robert Cray" Omnibus Press, 2000

Santelli, Robert. "The Big Book of Blues: The Fully Revised and Updated Biographical Encyclopedia" Penguin, 2001

Ward, Geoffrey C. and Ken Burns. "Jazz: A History of America's Music" Alfred A. Knopf, 2000

Weissman, Dick. "Blues, the Basics" Routledge, Taylor & Francis Group, 2005

Practice materials

Aebersold, Jamey. "Volume 2 Nothin' But Blues" Jamey Aebersold Jazz

Aebersold, Jamey. "Volume 42 Blues in All Keys" Jamey Aebersold Jazz

Haerle, Dan. "The Jazz Language" Alfred Music

Hal Leonard: The Blues, Jazz Play-Along, Volume 3

Hal Leonard: Blues Play-Along Series, Volumes 1- 6

Hal Leonard: Blues' Best, Jazz Play-Along Volume 30

Levine, Mark. "The Jazz Theory Book" Sher Music

Stoloff, Bob. "Blues Scatitudes: Vocal Improvisations of the Blues" Gerard & Sarzin Publishing Co.

Weir, Michele. "Fearless Vocal Improvisation" Advance Music

Songbooks

"The Blues Fake Book" Hal Leonard

"The Blues Fakebook" Woody Mann, Oak Publications

"The Blues Singer" Creative Concepts

"Sing Jazz!" Second Floor Music

DVDs

Alberta Hunter - Jazz Masters Series

All That Jazz: From New Orleans to New York

B.B. King: Blues Session

The Blues: Bessie Smith (Mamie Smith, Ida Cox, Big Bill Broonzy, etc.)

Blues Masters - The Essential History of the Blues, (Starring: Leadbelly, Bessie Smith)

Blues Vocals - Carol Rodgers and Masta Edwards
Buddy Guy: Teachin' the Blues
Chicago Blues (Featuring Muddy Waters, Johnnie Lewis, Buddy Guy, Junior Wells, etc.)
Deep Blues: A Musical Pilgrimage to the Crossroads
Ella Fitzgerald Live in '57 & '63
The Guitar Of Big Bill Broonzy
Jazz : A Film By Ken Burns
Joe Williams - Jazz Masters Series
John Lee Hooker - Come and See About Me: The Definitive DVD
The Ladies Sing The Blues (Billie Holiday, Sarah Vaughan, Dinah Washington, Lena Horne, Peggy Lee, Ethel Waters, Ruth Brown, and many others)
Lightnin' Hopkins: Rare Performances 1960-1979
Learn to Sing the Blues - Gaye Adegbaoloa
Louis Jordan & His Tympanny Five
Martin Scorsese Presents The Blues
Muddy Waters: Classic Concerts
Ralph Gleasons's Jazz Casual: Dizzy Gillespie/Mel Tormé
Ralph Gleasons's Jazz Casual: Jimmy Witherspoon/ Jimmy Rushing
Sarah Vaughan and other Jazz Divas
The Search for Robert Johnson
Son House - Masters of the Country Blues
Tom Waits & Mose Allison - Soundstage

Nowadays, there are many ways to hear blues music via the internet; one doesn't even need to own a CD or DVD player. Just go online and use a search engine like Yahoo or Google, entering the name of the song or artist you're interested in, or check YouTube.com for videos and films. You can also join websites that share music, like Rhapsody.com, which charges a modest monthly fee, or check iTunes.com or Amazon.com to buy or listen to samples of blues performances.

ABOUT JUDY NIEMACK

"…She sings like an angel, or at least like an angel who's heard Basie and Miles: she's got intonation that whole choruses would kill for, and a voice that never loses its soft sheen even at hot tempos and high volume. She's one of the few singers who actually should sing scat solos, since she thinks so much like a horn player."

Niel Tesser, Downbeat

"It seems only appropriate that Judy Niemack spends a significant amount of her time teaching, for there isn't anyone—whether jazz neophyte or veteran—who can't learn from her.... Niemack represents jazz singing at its finest and most accomplished. Throughout her two-decade career, she has consistently bordered on flawless, yet she's never become mannered or predictable".

Christopher Louden, Jazztimes

Born and raised in Pasadena, California, Judy gained her first musical experience singing in her church choir. She first heard jazz through her mother's Nancy Wilson records, and discovered that she could easily sing harmonies when she and her sister sang background vocals behind her brother, who played guitar and sang lead. As a child and as a teenager, she sang in a wide variety of settings including musical theatre productions, rock bands, folk music groups, and in a vocal jazz quartet

Judy studied classical singing, but the turning point in her studies occurred when she met the great tenor saxophonist Warne Marsh. "I became Warne's first vocal student. He treated me like a horn player. He assigned me solos by Charlie Parker, Roy Eldridge and others to learn. I learned about improvising from him. He called it instant composition." Judy studied classical singing at the New England Conservatory and the Cleveland Institute of Music. Moving to New York in 1977, she continued her studies with Marsh. This relationsip proved to be extremey valuable on the New York scene: Judy performed for a week with Marsh at the Village Vanguard in her first major appearance. She made her recording debut, leading the first of her eleven CDs, "By Heart," for the Sea Breeze label, which documented her association with the saxophonist.

"During that period, I was strictly an improviser, with no thought given to entertaining. But eventually, I started to focus on communicating through the lyrics, and then I really grew as a singer." Starting in the late 1970s, Judy began to work more regularly as a lyricist, and wrote lyrics to Clifford Brown's *Daahoud,* Thelonious Monk's *Misterioso,* Bill Evans' *Interplay,* Richie Powell's *Time* and Duke Jordan's *Jordu,* and songs by the likes of Lee Konitz, Pat Metheny, Dexter Gordon, Gigi Gryce, Elmo Hope, Kenny Dorham, Curtis Fuller, Bob Brookmeyer, Idrees Sulieman, Richie Beirach, Don Grolnick, Steve Slagle, Mike Stern, Johnny Griffin and many others. She has set herself apart as a writer through her focus on creating lyrics that are relevant to the contemporary jazz vocalist.

Her beautiful voice, fearless improvising, impressive musicianship and versatility has allowed her to perform with many of the giants of jazz, including Kenny Barron, George Benson, Dave Brubeck, David Byrne, Billy Higgins, Eddie Gomez, Peter Herbolzheimer, Fred Hersch, Lee Konitz, Joe Lovano, Clark Terry, Toots Thielemans, the New York Voices, Mal Waldron and Kenny Werner.

Judy Niemack started teaching jazz voice and improvisation in the late 1970s. She has since become one of the most influential educators in jazz, and a pioneer of vocal jazz education in Europe. She taught vocal jazz at the New School For Jazz, William Patterson University, Long Island University, New York City College and the Janice Borla Vocal Jazz Camp for twenty years. After moving to Europe, she joined the jazz faculty at the Royal Conservatory of Brussels, Belgium, in 1993. Two years later, she became the first Professor of Vocal Jazz at what is now the Jazz Institut Berlin in Germany. She currently holds a Guest

Professorship at Musikene Conservatory in San Sebastian, Spain, and leads workshops throughout the world.

Judy Niemack has accomplished a formidable body of work as a singer, educator, lyricist, and composer. She is an inspiration to younger jazz vocalists, and with all that she has done thus far, she still gives the impression that the best is yet to come. "I love standards and have performed them all of my life, but this is a new era and it is time to create new music. I'm open to all forms of vocal improvisation; I'm interested in mastering the art of music and raising the bar in vocal jazz performance." In this, her latest book, she explores the rich history of blues.

For more information, visit www.judyniemack.com.

DISCOGRAPHY

AS A LEADER

By Heart featuring Warne Marsh, Eddie Gomez (Seabreeze, 1978)

Blue Bop featuring Cedar Walton, Curtis Fuller, Ray Drummond, Joey Baron (Freelance, 1988)

Long as You're Living featuring Joe Lovano, Fred Hersch, Billy Hart (Freelance, 1990)

Heart's Desire duet with Kenny Barron (Stash, 1991)

Straight Up featuring Toots Thielemans, Kenny Werner, Adam Nussbaum, Mark Feldman, Jeanfrançois Prins (Freelance, 1993)

Mingus, Monk and Mal duet with Mal Waldron (Freelance, 1994)

. . . Night and the Music featuring Jeanfrançois Prins, Kenny Werner, Ray Drummond, Billy Hart, Eric Friedlander (Freelance, 1996)

About Time featuring Eddie Gomez, Jeanfrançois Prins, Lee Konitz, David Friedman, Edson da Silva (Café) (Sony Jazz, 2003)

What's Goin' On featuring Peter Herbolzheimer & Big Band Jazz Terrassa (Temps Record, 2005)

Blue Nights featuring Jeanfrançois Prins, Jim McNeely, Dennis Irwin, Victor Lewis, Gary Bartz, Don Sickler (BluJazz Productions, 2007)

In The Sundance featuring Bruce Barth, Rufus Reid, Jeanfrançois Prins, Bruno Castellucci (BluJazz Productions, 2009)

AS A GUEST (SELECTED DISCOGRAPHY)

Beauty and the Prince with Jeanfrançois Prins featuring Fred Hersch, Hein van de Geyn, Bruno Castellucci (AMC, 1993)

Rhapsody Volumes 1 and 2 with Lee Konitz (Paddle Wheel, 1993)

The Other Side of Walter Boeykens (distributed by Sony, 1994)

For more new recordings by Judy, of her music and lyrics, visit
www.JazzSingersCorner.com

Judy Niemack's lyrics used in this book were written to the following instrumental compositions.

A Shot of Blues Juice; Norman Simmons' **Blue Juice** was recorded by Norman Simmons on "Ramira The Dancer" (Spotlight 13) and by Al Grey on "Al Meets Bjarne" (Gemini 62)

The Count Is Back: Johnny Griffin's **Blues for Dracula** recorded by Philly Joe Jones on "Blues For Dracula" (Riverside 230)

New Concept (for a Blue Planet): Gigi Gryce's **Blue Concept** was recorded by Clifford Brown on "Complete Clifford Brown Big Band in Paris" (Vogue 7001); by Donald Byrd and Gigi Gryce on "Jazz Lab" (Columbia 998); by Art Farmer on "When Farmer Met Gryce" (Prestige 7085) and on "Farmer's Market" (Prestige 2032)

Run Home: Dexter Gordon's **Home Run** was recorded by Dexter Gordon on "The Resurgence Of Dexter Gordon" (Jazzland 929)

Eros: Julian Priester's **Blue for Eros** was recorded by Art Blakey on "Moanin'" (LaserLightJazz 17 127)

The Meeting: Johnny Griffin's **Camp Meeting** was recorded by Johnny Griffin on "Blues Up And Down" (Jazzland 60)

Blues That Soothe My Soul: Norman Simmons' **Blues to Soothe** has not been recorded instrumentally

Over the Brink: Julian Priester's **Push Come to Shove** has not been recorded instrumentally

For more great vocal jazz material, including downloadable PDF lead sheets and accompaniment-only audio, go to www.jazzleadsheets.com and visit the Singers' Corner or just go to www.JazzSingersCorner.com.

Other books by Judy Niemack
"Hear It and Sing It! Exploring Modal Jazz" (Second Floor Music) - includes a CD with Judy illustrating the exercises as well as accompaniment-only tracks.

"Jazz Vocal Standards" Pro Vocal Women's Edition Volume 18 (Hal Leonard Corp.) - includes CD

"Sing JAZZ! Leadsheets for 76 Jazz Vocals" (Second Floor Music) - includes *I'm Movin' On* by Kirk Nurock and Judy Niemack

"Jazz Phrasing: A Workshop for the Jazz Vocalist" Gloria Cooper, Don Sickler (Second Floor Music) - contains a section that explores different musical environments for *Movin' On* by Kirk Nurock and Judy Niemack; a CD with Judy illustrating the various approaches, plus practice tracks, is included.

Acknowledgments

My heartfelt thanks to all of the musicians who helped to broaden the blues palette presented here and to my fellow vocalists Mark Murphy, Darmon Meader, and Sheila Jordan: it was a joy to work with you! Special thanks to Jeanfrançois Prins for his patience, feedback and musical judgment and to Don Sickler for his musicianship, faith in the project, attention to detail ("I think it's bway, not bwih . . .") and for saying, "Hey Judy, how about a lyric to this one?"

Hear It and Sing It: Exploring the Blues CD
Vocalists Sheila Jordan, Darmon Meader, Mark Murphy and Judy Niemack
Pianists Bruce Barth, Jim McNeely and Norman Simmons
Guitarist Jeanfrançois Prins
Bassists Dennis Irwin and John Webber
Drummers Victor Lewis and Kenny Washington
Trumpeter Don Sickler

Recording, mixing and mastering: Rudy Van Gelder, Van Gelder Recording Studio, Inc., Englewood Cliffs, NJ.

All tracks recorded and mixed by Rudy Van Gelder except *Since You've Gone, Something to Say, Summer Blues* and *Ice White Blues*, which were recorded and mixed by Michael Broby, Acoustic Recording., Brooklyn, NY

Author: Judy Niemack
Producers: Don Sickler, Judy Niemack & Jeanfrançois Prins
Music editor: Don Sickler
Text editor: Cassie van Stolk-Cooke
Cover photos and cover design: Terry Chamberlain
Book design & completion: Maureen Sickler
Music engraving: Osho Endo
Photographers: Next Photo, Berlin (Judy Niemack); Jos Knaeppen (Dennis Irwin); Sud des Alpes (Sheila Jordan); Alfonse Pagano (Darmon Meader); Jean-Pierre Leduc (Mark Murphy)

Bassist Dennis Irwin was the first musician I called when I started recording the songs for this book. Sadly for the jazz community, he passed away in 2008. He was witty, eloquent, erudite and a masterful musician. I'm happy that, with this book, future generations of vocalists will be able to sing with him.

Thanks to the singers!

Sheila Jordan

Darmon Meader

Mark Murphy

YOU CAN STUDY WITH JUDY NIEMACK!

"Niemack represents jazz singing at its finest and most accomplished. Throughout her two-decade career, she has consistently bordered on flawless, yet she's never become mannered or predictable. It seems only appropriate that Judy Niemack spends a significant amount of her time teaching, for there isn't anyone--whether jazz neophyte or veteran--who can't learn from her."

Christopher Louden, *Jazztimes*

Judy Niemack's schedule of workshops and performances worldwide can be found at http://www.judyniemack.com.
Contact Judy there, where you can listen to more of her recorded music, download lyrics, register to take lessons online or purchase books and CDs.

Explore Modal Jazz with Judy Niemack's **Hear It and Sing It! Exploring Modal Jazz**

Learn to improvise during live performances and be comfortable doing it. With **Exploring Modal Jazz** you'll become familiar with the color of each chord and the mode it implies, preparing you to move on to chord progressions. The accompanying CD makes getting started simple: no matter where you are, just play the CD from the begining and sing along to learn by ear the easy way. The CD explores the basic concepts of vocal improvisation: singing the scales with their complimentary chords, developing melodic motifs and becoming comfortable with common scat syllables while feeling the rhythmic grooves.

It's a fun and effective way to improve your vocal technique and internalize the basic scales used in jazz..

Available from Hal Leonard Music Dispatch (1-800-637-2852) or your local music dealer.
HL00001001 Hear It and Sing It! Exploring Modal Jazz with Judy Niemack

---

jazz lead sheets & more
jazzleadsheets.com

THE Singers' Corner

Visit **SingersCorner.com** at www.jazzleadsheets.com

It's an exciting place where jazz vocalists can get vocal lead sheets by great jazz composers: new music by contemporary composers and lyricists as well as many classic instrumental titles, now with lyrics. Hear clips of the new lyric versions as well as the original instrumentals. Buy the complete lyric performance for download. Often, an accompaniment-only version is available in mp3 format to help you learn.

Get the PDF lead sheet in the offered key, or request one in your own key.

Practice the new chart, get tips on how to arrange it for your band, and be ready for the next gig.

Expand your repertoire at
www.jazzleadsheets.com!